CU01278842

ON THE EDGE OF

THORNHILL AND ITS ENVIRONS: A SOCIAL HISTORY REVISITED

Stuart McCulloch

A Thornhill Community Trust publication.
First published in 1995 by the Munro Trust in
association with Stirling Libraries

This edition published in 2018 by the Thornhill Community Trust

© Stuart McCulloch

All rights reserved. No part of this publication may be reproduced, stored in
a retrieval system, or transmitted in any form, or by any means, electronic or
otherwise without prior permission of the author.

ISBN 978-15272-2905-1

Typeset by laytxt, Glasgow

Printed in Glasgow by Bell & Bain Limited

In loving memory of Anne McCulloch

Contents

Contents

Contents

List of Illustrations

Front Cover Design Stewart Campbell
Back Cover *Thornhill Cross Roads* Henry Morley (1869–1937), (from the collections of the Stirling Smith Art Gallery and Museum)

PART ONE

PART TWO

List of Illustrations

PART THREE

Maps Acknowledgements

Fig. 8 District map (John Adair c. 1680), Fig. 12 Edgar's survey map 1746,
Fig. 16 John Thomson's map of western Perthshire 1832,
Fig. 33 Village map 1887 (Ordnance Survey) all reproduced by kind
permission of the National Library of Scotland.
Fig. 14 Roy's military maps of Scotland, c. 1752, 2 sheets, ©British Library.

Foreword to the First Edition

When I came to stay in the village a few short years ago my initial perceptions, perhaps similar to those of the passers-by, were quickly corrected. I found a lively integrated community, happy to welcome newcomers yet complete in its self-confidence. When research undertaken by the Regional Archivist unearthed details of the foundation of the village three hundred years ago plans quickly unfolded for a year long series of celebrations and activities. As part of this I agreed to compile a history of our community to coincide with the year of the Tercentenary.

As research proceeded certain themes emerged which, I believe, can play a small part in understanding the life of small Scottish communities. The early years brought more than a fair share of conflict and change, because the area enjoyed a position near Stirling, the central 'buckle' of Scotland. Early communications, especially the fords, also tended to direct attention towards the local area. However following the Industrial Revolution the area found itself rather isolated, as the railways became the dominant factor in growth. Therefore there is the opportunity of studying the development of a village built upon long and firm foundations but missing out on the rapid growth that affected many of the small settlements of Central Scotland.

Historical writing is full of dangers and pitfalls, mainly because we are writing about people and events of which we have no personal knowledge. So I have probably made mistakes and for these I apologise in advance. Historical details have been cross checked wherever possible but nevertheless there is a place in this book for oral tales that cannot be substantiated by documentation. I make no apologies for including such tales. A bigger problem is deciding what to exclude and I hope the many contributors will be able to forgive me if have omitted what I should not have. The fault is entirely my own.

Primary sources, principally from the Central Regional Council, The Scottish Records Office, Edinburgh and The Central Region Archives in Stirling and Perth yielded a great deal of information, as did the excellent University of Stirling Library and the Smith Museum. I gratefully acknowledge all the help received from the staff at these locations and I must particularly thank Elma Lindsay of the Smith Gallery and Lorna Main from the Central Regional Council Archaeological Services.

Every community has a rich seam of historical data just waiting to be discovered and Thornhill is certainly no exception. Many of the long term residents gave invaluable help in providing information. I cannot list all the helpful people that have given advice, assistance and encouragement but I must record my particular thanks to Ian Bain, Jean Buchanan, Cissy Craig, John Dick, Mary Diggins, William Dawson, Tona Fitches, Annie Taylor, Hamish McLachlan, John Millar, Robin Price, Betty Spence, Donald Mac-Farlane and Betty Paterson. During the course of research Mr. Bob Hendry passed away. Bob was one of the genuine village characters with a huge fund of stories. He will be greatly missed by all of us, and I am glad that I was able to record a few of his tales for the future. Mr. and Mrs. Dick of Hillhead gave unselfishly of their time and wisdom and in allowing me to explore the writings of the Reverend Williams when he was the UF Minister, I was able to gain a great deal of fascinating information collected almost 100 years ago. I am also grateful to Sheila Scott of the Biggar Museum for sharing with me her research on the Buchan family that enabled me to make the connection of John Buchan to Thornhill. For their editing and administration many thanks go to Barbara Thorp, Anne McCulloch, Kirsty McCulloch, William Dawson, Willie Rae and Isobel Rae. Michael Giannandrea of Stirling Libraries has been unstinting in his support and deserves grateful appreciation.

This short history can only introduce the story of the people who have lived and enjoyed the village of Thornhill and the parish community of Norrieston. The pleasure of the unfolding story has all been mine.

Preface to the Second Edition

Over twenty years have passed since the first edition of the 'History of Thornhill and its environs'. The first edition was produced at speed, under a strict deadline, notably the tercentenary of the establishment of the village of Thornhill.

Much has changed. Fortunately a great deal of new material has come to light and in many ways this is a new book. I have added some new sections, reorganised the content, gone a little deeper into some of the themes previously covered and hopefully amended any inaccuracies that sadly crept into the first edition.

It remains essentially a social history and hence looks at the activities of the people who have lived here, both before and after the establishment of the village itself. This makes the definition of the boundaries important but also rather subjective. Thornhill village is at the centre but the book also explores the surrounding area, bounded by the rivers Teith in the north and Forth in the south. It stretches eastwards to include Blair Drummond and westwards to include Ruskie and Blairhoyle, all very important areas, especially in the pre-Thornhill days.

There have been some important developments over the past 20 years or so. George Dixon's 1995 publication of the establishment of Thornhill kicked off everything and since then a number of important studies have taken place, especially MacNiven's study of place names and Harrison's detailed exploration of Flanders Moss. The boundary of the Loch Lomond and Trossachs National Park lies only a few miles away and the significance of the history and heritage of the area featured in this book has been recognised by the establishment of the Thornhill Conservation Area and the many listed buildings present.

None of this would be of great consequence were it not for the dynamism of local activists. A myriad of community groups and activities continue in the village. In particular the team who produce Thornhill Community Trust's community newsletter, 'Thornhill Views' (TV) has done wonderful work recently maintaining a strong interest in local heritage. In turn they have done much to maintain the strong community feel which has been a hallmark of the village for over 300 years.

I am, of course, rather biased, because they have given me the opportunity to update and compile this volume, a task which gives me enormous pride and pleasure. I hope the reader can share this sentiment with me.

Ackowledgements

In the shadows behind every history book stands a battalion of helpers and well-wishers and this book is most certainly no exception. If the level of voluntary support is an indication of the strength of a community then Thornhill and its environs can stand proud.

The inspiration for this book came from the Thornhill Community Trust and their sub-committee of volunteers have consistently risen to every challenge they have faced. In particular, my thanks go to the hard-working and ever helpful Stewart Campbell, David Firth, Archie Paterson, Peter Rickard and Fiona MacDougall.

I was fortunate to be able to add a great deal of new material to this volume and for this my gratitude goes to all the many contributors and helpers who assisted locally and nationally. They include Neil Aitkenhead, Kate Anderson, Roddy Anderson, Christine Bauer, Elaine and James Blanchard, Jean Cowie, Sue Duke, Norma Hall, Charlotte Johnston, James Kennedy, Elspeth King, Susie McCarron, Belinda MacMillan, Sir John MacMillan, Hamish McLachlan, The National Library of Scotland, The National Archives of Scotland, Otago Settlers Museum, Ewan Reilly, Gary Richardson, Lynne Rickard, Marian Robb, Kate Sankey, The Stirling Council Community Pride Fund, The Stirling Council Mobile Library Service, The Stirling Smith Art Gallery and Museum, Stirling University Library Staff, Charlotte Smith, Thornhill & Blair Drummond Community Council, Heather Westwood, Ewan Wilson, Libby Yule and all the many others who are not directly mentioned here.

I would not have been able to write this book without the support of my long-suffering wife, Maureen. Thanks Maureen-maybe we will go on holiday soon?

Proof reading and checking is time consuming and can also be a thankless task. Let me ensure that our wonderful proof readers, notably Roddy Anderson, David Firth, Joyce Firth, Fiona MacDougall, Duncan McCulloch, Archie Paterson, Heather Westwood and Charlotte Smith are fully appreciated for all their time, effort and expertise. Any mistakes are purely mine.

Finally, I must gratefully acknowledge the driving force behind this book. The indefatigable Joyce Firth has chaired all our meetings, juggled all the various strands and never once took her eye off the objective. How she has continued to direct, cajole and encourage everyone without losing temper and patience has been a joy to behold.

About the Author

Stuart McCulloch is an award-winning historian and author of the first edition of *Thornhill and its Environs* (1995). He has recently published *A Scion of Heroes*, a biography of Captain James Murray, the Napoleonic War naval hero.

Stuart spent his undergraduate years at Queen Mary College, University of London and holds research degrees from both Stirling University and Glasgow University. He was Deputy Headmaster at the former Beaconhurst School in Bridge of Allan and then Headmaster at Belmont School, Newton Mearns.

He is married to Maureen and has three grown-up children and lots of dogs. He now spends his time cycling around the country and writing and lecturing about things long past.

Part One

The Early Years

Fig. 1 The Burnbank Green Man

1

On the Edge?

IT IS ALL TOO EASY FOR PASSERS-BY TO RUSH through the village
of Thornhill with the hills of Loch Lomond and the Trossachs
National Park beckoning impatiently to them. Perhaps the hand-
some cottages and houses lining the Main Street hardly get a second
glimpse. However, behind the facade of the houses lies a tale; in
fact, very many tales. This small village was once considered (erroneously) to be almost at the geographical centre of Scotland but it
would be more accurate to look at Thornhill as on the edge; between
mountain and moss land, between highland and lowland, between
Pict and Scot, between Highland Gael and Lowlander and between
industrialisation and traditional life. Life on the edge is rarely dull,
so this small part of Scotland was able to bestow its hidden tales
and secrets; and there were plenty of them.

It was the physical geography of the area that underpinned so
many of the incidents and episodes that follow. Thornhill only
entered recorded history in 1696 but the terrain which now makes
up the village and surrounding lands had been occupied for thousands of years. It has a dual character as befits a borderland. To the
south and east is the flat low-lying Forth Valley but to the north and
west lie the hills and mountains of Highland Scotland. The Highland Boundary Fault runs from Helensburgh in the south west as
far as Stonehaven in the north east and this fault line border runs
close by. Its effect on history has been acute, determining not only
the agricultural and economic activity either side of the boundary
but also acting as a linguistic and cultural frontier.

Combine this geological fault with the effects of glaciation and
the present landscape starts to emerge. When the glaciers which
ran from the north and west gradually retreated much of the land
that was to become the Forth Valley flooded and over time left
behind a thick deposit of clay that now sits above sea-level. The
result today is a fertile valley but one that until the late 18th century was a blanket of peat moss in many parts. Yet there are some

ridges of higher land that break through the moss, rising as raised beaches and terminal moraines, many of which lie to the east and

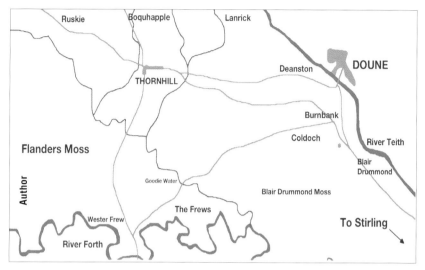

Fig. 2 Situation and landmarks around Thornhill

south of the Lake of Menteith. Thornhill itself makes use of one of these raised beaches, lying at a height of about 33 feet.

Human settlement was not easy but numerous prehistoric remains have been recorded which testify to the activity of people in our area. Alas, few now remain. A ceremonial burial mound, probably for local people of high status, is situated at Blair Drummond, west of the current caravan park site. It is a substantial tree covered mound from the bronze or neolithic age. An excavation in the 1920s found two cist burials and a cremation in a bronze age pot. Archaeologists consider that there may be many more burials below the mound believing that this was a site of some importance. Similarly at Craighead Lodge another sizeable prehistoric burial mound can be seen. An early excavation of 1758 testified a recovery of 'urns', but material evidence is no longer to be seen.

Ancient man revered their dead but there is evidence hereabouts of the living too. Prehistoric settlements, which may have taken the form of a roundhouse, often with a palisade defence structure, can be found at Cardona, Spittalton, Craighead, East Coldoch (2), Blaircessnock and East Torrie. Today they can mainly be spotted as crop marks and no doubt there were many many more, now lost to view.

Larger structures, with a primary defence function, such as 'duns' arrived with the Celts in about the 7th century BC and their use, in some cases, continued into the Middle Ages. The early duns had near vertical ramparts that were built from stone and timber and often two walls, an inner wall and an outer one. They usually took the form of a hillfort and three local ones have been identified at East Torrie, Easter Borland and West Torrie. A further fort/dun can be found at Tamnafalloch, Ruskie.

In the far North and the Outer Isles there are numerous examples of circular structures known as brochs. These were up to sixty feet high and contained a circular courtyard with passages and rooms built into the huge thickness of wall enclosing their centre. Their origins are unclear and even their dates of construction are open to debate. Some researchers date them as early as 300–350 BC but most have suggested more recent times, perhaps at the end of the Roman Occupation or even later. More than 500 broch sites are known or suspected. The vast majority are concentrated in the areas north of the Great Glen but they are rather more unusual away from north and west Scotland. Surprisingly, there are at least two, the Brae of Boquhapple and Coldoch, within three miles of Thornhill.

The remains of the broch at the Brae of Boquhapple are believed to be 1800–2200 years old. The central mound, 98 feet in diameter was enclosed in a double earth and stone bank and fronted by ditches on the north, south and west with the Cessintully Burn providing protection to the east. It is considered a good example of a southern broch, especially with its surviving outworks.

The best preserved of the local brochs is at Coldoch, where it stands on a slight rise immediately above the flat moss land of the Forth Valley. This scheduled ancient monument, although now in very poor condition, has deteriorated considerably in living memory and testimonies assert that one chamber was still roofed early in the 20th century. Its circular wall, of poor quality masonry, measures between seventeen and nineteen feet in thickness, although it is only five or six feet high now. There are three little chambers off the main centre at basement level and the two feet wide entrance was secured by a bar. The slot for this bar is seven feet deep. An old

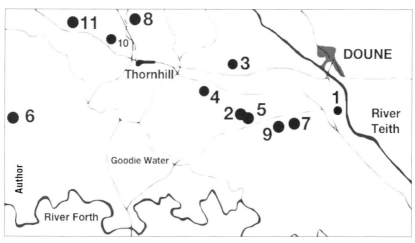

Fig. 3 Prehistoric sites

Burial Mounds:	**1** Blair Drummond **2** Craighead Lodge
Enclosures:	**3** Cardona. **4** Spittalton **5** Craighead **6** Blaircessnock
	7 East Coldoch (2)
Brochs:	**8** Brae of Boquhapple **9** Coldoch
Duns:	**10** Easter Borland **11** Tamnafalloch

stairway is recognisable within the wall. It may be that the site of this broch was coastal when it was built and fragments of whale-bones are reported to have been found inside it. The Forth Valley was once a shallow estuary of the sea and Coldoch broch would have been close to this former estuary. Whales were doubtless occasionally stranded in the shallow water.

The occurrence of brochs outside the main area to the north has been linked with the Roman invasion. One theory is that their construction resulted from the migration of broch builders from the north to form an alliance with the Caledonii on their southern frontiers to act as a buffer against the Roman forces. It has also been suggested that they were built to order by groups of professional broch building engineers. Certainly, Roman occupation was brief and has left few artefacts and remains; the sum total being a rudimentary Roman road passing through the area from Stirling to Gartmore, perhaps a Roman outpost on Keir Hill at Auchensalt

Farm and a probable temporary Roman camp at Netherton.

The Torwood broch, south of Stirling is very similar to Coldoch and it has been suggested that these two were built at a different time, either earlier or later, than the other Forth Valley brochs, and probably by a group of people who had no contact with the Romans. Archaeologists have argued for a post-Roman date, perhaps in the later second or in the early third century and after any local Roman influence had disappeared. A professional broch designer may have been recruited to design Coldoch (and Torwood) and to supervise its construction, although the broch occupants were part of the local native population and they may have learned the technical skills required to build their brochs.

Although there is often little to see today, these brochs indicate that the area must have had a substantial settled population at a time when the possibility of attack was ever present. Local

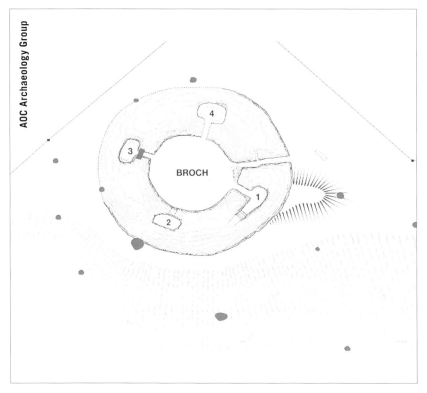

Fig.4 Coldoch Broch plan

Fig. 5 Coldoch Broch entrance passage, facing east

The remains of this unusual local broch were much more prominent within living memory.

inhabitants on hearing of an invasion would flee to their broch where (they hoped) they would have a measure of protection against the marauders.

Amongst the post-Roman groups who may have constituted these marauders were the Strathclyde Britons, the Picts and later, the Scots. If the later date for the Coldoch construction is accepted it adds strength to the argument that this area is 'at the edge'; this time between the Strathclyde Britons with their capital of Dumbarton and the Pictish kingdoms to the north and east. The kingdom of Strathclyde's territorial extent incorporated the modern county of Dunbartonshire and western Stirlingshire and included the area surrounding Loch Lomond. The local area, part of the region to become known as Menteith, is situated to the east of that kingdom, between Loch Lomond and Stirling. To the north of Menteith was the earldom of Strathearn, which was certainly a Pictish territory. To the east was Clackmannanshire and Fife, also both Pictish. Thus Menteith was to remain 'at the crossroads' for many hundreds of years as Picts, Gaels, Britons, Angles and Vikings battled for local supremacy.

Most of the evidence of these earlier groups is based upon place-name analysis. In Strathclyde the inhabitants spoke a p-Celtic language, similar in form to modern Welsh. The Pictish groups had a different language or at least a different form of the language and this varied from the British of Strathclyde and from the Gaelic of the Scots. Menteith itself is probably of p-Celtic origin. Its earliest written forms are Meneteth and Meneted dating from the mid-1160s and perhaps derived from the British 'mönïð', a word related to (Welsh) mynydd or (Cornish) menedh, meaning 'mountain or rough grazing'.[1]

Was Menteith part of 'Pictland' as is sometimes assumed? On nearby Dumyat was the 'fort of the Maeatae', probably the centre of a British stronghold. Furthermore, there seems to be nothing inherently Pictish about Menteith; there are no Pictish symbol stones and no 'pett'-names, (Pictish meaning 'land-holding' and frequently found in place-names on former Pictish territory). To counter this argument Menteith was part of the diocese of Dunblane and there was an attack on Dunblane by the Britons of Strathclyde in the second quarter of the 9th century, suggesting that the city was occupied by Picts or possibly by this date, the Gaels.

MacNiven,[2] in his study of Menteith placenames concluded that some questions remain to be explored more fully and there is a great deal of difficulty in distinguishing between the Pictish and British languages on place-name evidence alone. However, he argued that if there is a boundary to be drawn in relation to Pictish and British on the basis of place names and political geography, this boundary would be not at the river Forth, but rather at the uplands to the north of Doune and Callander, on the northern boundaries of Menteith. Any movement between the two power centres of Strathclyde and Pictland would have to cross the Forth and the great mosses bordering it. The predominant crossing place above Stirling is likely to have been what ultimately became well-known as the 'Fords of Frew', to the south of present day Thornhill. Traffic here will have intensified as Christianity extended its influence throughout the kingdoms; it has been suggested that Menteith was a major routeway on the journey from Iona to Lindisfarne for Gaels travelling

---

[1] MacNiven, 2011

[2] *ibid*

between these two important Christian centres.

Perhaps the travelling Gaels awakened a more unhealthy interest in the area from the Dalriada Scots of Argyll, who were themselves under pressure from invading Vikings. According to the Annals of Ulster, Aedán mac Gabráin, king of Dalriada, won a major battle locally in 582 AD and a fort near Aberfoyle is traditionally said to have been given to St Berchán or Berach by the victorious Aedán to become the site of a monastery. Aedán in an early poem was referred to as a prince or king of 'Foirthe' which would connect him to the Forth region and suggest he was well established in the area. Certainly by 1100 Menteith had experienced a change in its cultural identity which had brought to an end the era of Picts and Britons as the dominant peoples in the locality. The Dalriada Scots had prevailed and their language, Scots Gaelic, was to become established as the overriding spoken language of the area thus replacing the British and Pictish tongues that had previously prevailed.

2

Home is Where the Heart is: Where They Lived

A LTHOUGH THORNHILL WAS NOT TO FEATURE ON the landscape map until 1696 people had been living in the local area for millennia. Maybe that was a surprise, as the area on first sight did not have a lot going for it. Hemmed in by rivers, the Teith to the north and the Forth to the south, the bit in-between was principally covered by an almost impassable bog and moss land; a district to act as a barrier rather than a catalyst for trade and transport. The more populated lowlands were faraway places, accessible only by track and travel through difficult country containing hidden dangers for the unaware.

But that did not tell the full story. For those in the know there were hidden ways. Gaps through the moss, passes through the hills and fords across the rivers served to converge the early travellers and focus them on the area later to become known as the parishes of Kincardine, Kilmadock and Port of Menteith. They were strategically well placed and history was not going to pass by unnoticed. Prior to the draining of the moss lands, a route of great importance ran along the southern side of the carselands via Gargunnock, Kippen and on to Dumbarton. By 1646, perhaps even much earlier, there was a corresponding although much less important route north of the Forth linking Blair Drummond with Port of Menteith and Aberfoyle and passing sites such as Burnbank, Coldoch, Spittalton, Boquhapple and Ruskie.

For north-south routes, the Forth was a significant barrier. The bridge at Stirling, for hundreds of years the lowest bridging point of the Forth, was of great prominence. It was a toll road and was near to the garrisons of Stirling Castle so any river crossing with an objective of economy or mischief would be forced to look elsewhere and this usually meant the fords at Frew. The fords in early times were famous and it was said that they were known in the medieval era as one of the 'seven wonders of Scotland', perhaps referring to a construction built by Kenneth MacAlpín and noted in the Chronicle of the Kings of Alba before 995:

And Kenneth walled the banks of the fords of Forthin

where Forthin could be an early form for Frew. The name Frew is from the Gaelic 'na Friùthachan' which in turn derives from the Brittonic 'frwd' meaning a current or a shallow spot in a fairly deep river. There may have been more than one ford here hence the several present day placenames containing 'frew'.

The fords are usually situated near where the Boquhan Burn meets the River Forth and so located in a place where the alluvium and silt from the burn would build up. That they were well used is confirmed many times in history, ranging from mentions by the retreating troops after the battle of Sauchieburn to the antics of Rob Roy MacGregor and the army of Charles Edward Stuart.

The fords at Frew were confined to history in the early 19th century when they were superseded by a bridge with a new route constructed to Thornhill. Prior to that the route had veered north east through the Lands of Frew, onto the Bridge of Goodie (on record by 1646) and finally linking with other communications at Doune and the river Teith.

An intriguing placename which may indicate that visitors did traverse the area, perhaps for pilgrimage or for trade, is Spittal, which derives from the Latin 'hospitalaria' meaning 'the hostelry, a hospital or the guest house of a monastery'. There are several placenames with the element 'Spittal' in Menteith and locally Spittalton first appears on record in 1491 but there is a dilemma. Did the placename indicate the function of the centre or is it named after its inhabitants? Certainly by 1480 Gilchrist and John Spittale are mentioned locally and nearby Coldoch was certainly owned by Robert Spittal of Stirling in 1513, although his original mansion house has now been demolished. Robert Spittal was the favourite tailor of King James IV and had become renowned for his establishment of the hospital at Stirling and the bridges at Doune and Bannockburn. He owned the lands now called Spittalton and this may be the origin of the name. This doesn't negate the possibility of a small hospital or refuge at Spittalton and it is probable that one did exist here until at least 1500. The Spittal name often recurs in land records of the area; indeed their family was represented amongst the first families of the new Thornhill when James Spittal and his wife Agnes McKean took up a large feu containing several other existing buildings at the base of the Thornhill ridge towards the march with Norrieston, probably on the site where the Lion and Unicorn now stands.

Placenames are frequently used to give indications of the origin of a site and may help to understand social and language development through the ages. The language timeline moves from the earliest identifiable spoken language, Brittonic or p-Celtic, a language similar to modern Welsh, until the invasions of the Gaelic speaking Scots from Ireland led to Gaelic becoming the language used for the vast majority of the place-names prior to the 15th century. After this time Scots-English placenames became more common.

One of the earliest recognisable local placenames of p-Celtic or Brittonic origin is Lanrick. This has the element 'lanerc' from a word meaning a 'clearing in a wood'. From this we can infer that at least some land had been cleared for settlement by the time the Gaelic speaking Scots arrived in Menteith.

Menteith itself was one of the ancient provinces of Scotia[3] and written records first appear around 1164 when Gilbert, Earl of Menteith was listed as a witness to a charter at Scone Abbey. The name Menteith seems to be of a p-Celtic origin and thus also pre-dates the Gaelic speaking settlement of the area.

Narrowing down the geographical area to parish level, Kincardine puts in an appearance as early as 1189. 'Kin', a common constituent of many placenames, comes from the Gaelic 'ceann' meaning head or end and the second part of the word is the Pictish or Gaelic loan-word of 'carden', probably meaning woodland, although it may mean enclosure or encampment. The other local parish is Kilmadock which first appeared in records of 1275 and originates from the Gaelic 'cill' meaning church or religious place and 'docus', an early saint's name. This is examined in more detail in the background to the Dog family (*see page 32*).

Up until very recent times much of the land was divided into sizeable estates and they were owned by a relatively small number of 'lairds'. These lairds would have a number of tenants on their land

---

[3] Scotland north of the Forth and Clyde rivers

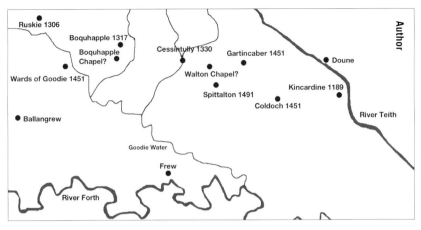

Fig. 6 Medieval settlement

and additionally the more established tenants would also employ landless labourers who worked for and with them. The two local estates which dominate the medieval and early modern periods are Ruskie and Boquhapple.

The estate of Ruskie, first mentioned in 1306, seemed to be a complicated yet sizeable piece of land which at its greatest extent stretched from Auchyle in the west, Loch Ruskie in the north (where it was the centre of a medieval barony) and south towards Cardross, itself another ancient and extensive estate.

The land tenure and extent of Boquhapple was even more intricate. As 'Bucopill' it first appeared in 1317 and was erroneously considered to be named after a local chapel of Inchmahome Priory. There is no direct written evidence to support this origin. The derivation of the place name is now considered to be from 'both' and 'chapaill' (the horse/mare shieling or bothy) and the area was perhaps an important horse-rearing area in the earlier Middle Ages.[4] Settlements using the name Boquhapple are situated almost three miles apart from north to south and in addition by 1330 the estate was also divided into Easter Boquhapple (including the land now occupied by Thornhill) and Wester Boquhapple. King's Boquhapple indicated land which was held by the crown following the forfeiture of land of the Stewart Menteiths. It is clear that this was an

---

[4] MacNiven, 2011

extensive and important estate and at various times it has been subdivided to different owners.

A similar scenario occurred in Cessintully, the neighbouring estate to the east. There is no large settlement today called Cessintully but the place name lives on in the Brae of Cessintully, Cessintully Mill and the Cessintully Burn (traditionally the march between Cessintully and Boquhapple). In medieval and early modern times a more sizeable settlement certainly existed. Cessintully (seskentuly) itself dates from 1330 and it may owe its origin to being an early meeting place (from the Gaelic 'tulach' meaning 'mound, place of assembly'). Certainly by 1509 it had grown to become a 'ville de Cessintuly' and by 1528 it was the 'baronia de Cessintulie'.

By this date the area was to feature a remarkable concentration of new names of Scots-English origin, all with the suffix 'toun'. A town in Scotland was called a 'burgh' but the suffix 'toun' describes a 'fermtoun', the dominant settlement and economic pattern of much of rural Scotland up to the 18th century. A fermtoun was a group farm shared by an extended family or by portioners in joint tenure and they were scattered across the landscape.

Some of the fermtouns may have grown into a small village size but most had only two to four families in main tenure together with a number of subtenants and cottars. Ramsay of Ochtertyre commented:

> as far as records go the Menteith area was divided into towns occupied by two or more tenants or cottages built very close together for defence against highlanders[5]

The earliest known Cessintully 'toun' was Donald-youngistoun which is on record by 1488–9. This disappeared when Donald Young's portion of Cessintully was sold. Baxtertoune is on record from 1541 as Baxtartoun. This metamorphosed somehow into Boghall, a name which it retains today. Other toun-names came on record in the 1520s but many of the surnames attached to them are found much earlier in the exchequer rolls. For example, the probable founder of Mackeanston is Donald McCane, who is on record from 1480 as a tenant in the 'lands of Sessintuly'. Thomas and

[5] Ramsay, J., *Scotland and Scotsmen in the Eighteenth Century*, 1888

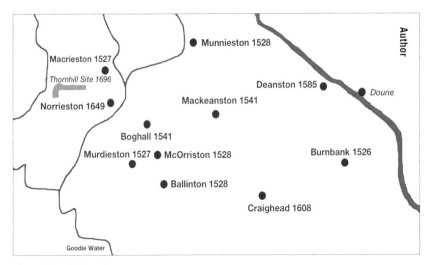

Fig. 7 The 'Touns'

Forsith McCorane are tenants in the lands of Cessintully in 1480 and founded McOrriston but the toun itself dates only from 1528. Mackrieston dates from 1527 and Munnieston is from 1528. This name may originate from the Gaelic word for monk, 'manach' and so this may have been land originally belonging to Inchmahome but there is no written record to confirm this. Murdieston dates from 1527 and may owe its origin to Murdach Smyth, a tenant of Cessintully from at least 1480 to 1488, or perhaps from Johannes Murthoson, who in 1484 was also a local tenant. Also in the running is Murthoch Kessokissone and Kessok Murthauson (father and son?), both tenants in Cessintully in 1486. Ballinton dates from 1528 but may not be a 'toun' name. An alternative derivation of this is 'baile na toine' (township of the backside), perhaps named from its situation on the very edge of the carse.

Other 'touns' such as Netherton are sub-divisions of existing places, in this case the 'lower toun' of either Norrieston or Boquhapple.

East of Cessintully is the ancient heartland of the Kincardine parish and over the centuries it has held a number of important estates. Holdings of significance, mainly of Gaelic origin, include Coldoch, Gartincaber, Burnbank, Spittalton, Cuthil Brae and Blair Drummond itself.

Coldoch is first recorded in 1451 and the estate, which may also have included Craighead and Spittalton, has been the home of a number of notable local families including the Muschets, the Dogs and the Norries (*see Chapter 3*).

Also once home to the Dog/Doig family was Gartincaber (from Gaelic 'gart nan cabar', an enclosed field or settlement near prominent tree trunks or poles, perhaps only partially cleared woodland). The Estate dates from 1451 and parts of the present house are of significant antiquity.

The estate of Burnbank, dating from 1526, is also of considerable significance. Although the Scots name is not ancient, this was the home of the important Muschet family who were to play such a large part in the early history of the district. There are still remains of the original Muschet tower house nearby as is also the grave of Margaret Drummond, who died of the plague in 1647 (*see Fig. 9*).

Nearby, Cuthil Brae has an even earlier pedigree. The name 'Cuthil' is probably from the Gaelic 'comhdhail', which means a place of assembly often tied up with the dispensing of justice. As it is also near to the site of a motte and the former Kincardine Castle its position supports such a function. The medieval motte here was a timber castle on top of a mound 26 feet high surrounded by a six foot wide ditch. This could date from the 11th century but may be a bit later. A similar although smaller motte is found at Keir, Mid Borland. Rather later but still medieval was the moated homestead at Ballangrew, believed to be a hunting lodge within Flanders Moss.

The main residence for the more recent owners of these Kincardine lands was situated to the south east of both Cuthil Brae and Burnbank. The earliest known owners of the Blair Drummond estates were the Muschet family, from whom the property was acquired by the Drummonds in 1364. They gradually amassed other lands and their mansion, Blair House, was completed in 1717 from a design of Alexander McGill. Henry Homes, Lord Kames, the famous land improver, formalised the gardens between 1766 and 1782 but wished for a contemporary house. It took a while. A new site was chosen on higher ground nearby and on its completion in 1872 the original house was demolished. Blair Drummond House is a listed category B baronial-style mansion built to a design of J.C. Walker. In 1975, the house and 17 acres of grounds were sold to the Camphill Trust as a Residential Home. The rest of the estate is still run commercially and includes a Safari Park and a caravan site.

The spiritual needs of Kincardine were served by the nearby parish church and the western part of the district was likely served by the chapel at Boquhapple maintained by the priory of Inchmahome. Associated with the chapel and a reader here in 1584 was Michael Learmonth and by 1594 Alexander Anderson was also to be involved.[6]

To the east there was an ancient monastery in the parish of Kilmadock and this had seven associated chapels. One was called 'Walton'. No trace of this exists today but evidence points to this being situated in the small glen between Boghall Farm and the Mill of Cessintully, east of the present village of Thornhill. This chapel was still in existence as late as 1720 where it is mentioned in kirk session records.

Maybe a motive for people settling nearby was the proximity of Christ's Well. The exact location of this well is unclear. Paterson in his 'History of Cambusbarron' maintains that this famous well was the Chapelwell of Cambusbarron, but the Reverend Williams in his extensive local research insists that the well was located in the parish of Kincardine and is likely to be associated with an early chapel. Wherever it was it had a huge impact on local people. Men and women for scores of miles around would carry home water in a stoup from this well because it was supposedly endowed with magical healing properties such as giving the power of sight to the blind and the healing of skin disorders, including the dreaded leprosy.

---

[6] Although McNiven (2011) asserts that he was unable to find documents which demonstrate a working chapel here in medieval times

3

The Good, the Bad and the Ugly

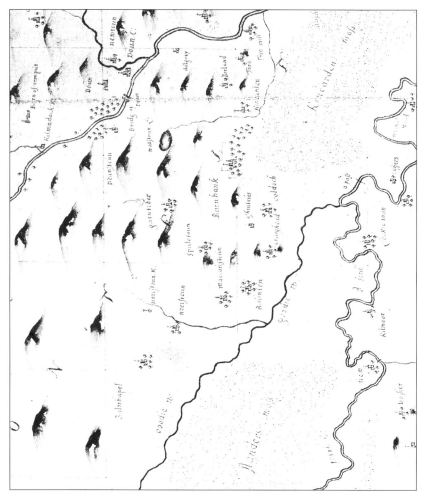

Fig. 8 District map (John Adair c. 1680)

This is probably the earliest map available, drawn just prior to the establishment of Thornhill in 1696. Note the extent of Flanders Moss and Kincardine Moss, demonstrating the strategic position of the future Thornhill which dominates the gap between the two moss areas.

S ADLY, EARLY HISTORICAL REFERENCES TEND TO FOCUS on the few local families who sat at the top of the social spectrum with references to their tenants and other local inhabitants being scarce. Even so, history has given us rich pickings; some of them were good, some were bad and some were both. No paintings or photographs are available to help us decide on the 'ugly' component but some of the events and actions which took place certainly merit the term.

The extant records demonstrate that local human activity was dominated by just a few families, notably the Stewart Earls of Menteith, the Drummonds, the Grahams, the Muschets, the Napiers, the Dogs and the Norries; and a colourful bunch they were!

The Earls of Menteith

By the 12th century the local area was a small constituent of the vast estates controlled by the Earls of Menteith. The first known Earl of Menteith was Gillecrist who comes on record in 1164 as a witness to a charter of Scone Abbey. Skipping to 1232 the powerful Comyn family entered Menteith, with the marriage of Walter Comyn, Lord of Badenoch to Isabella, the daughter of Earl Muirethach of Menteith. After Walter Comyn's death in 1258 the earldom passed to Walter Stewart, often known by his Gaelic nickname of Balloch, 'spotted'. By this time the Menteith Earls had risen in prestige and Walter had become prominent at the Scottish court. The family were to be serious players during the turmoil of the Wars of Independence and their participation ensured that the poor people of Menteith would suffer the agonies of warfare all too frequently.

When King Alexander III fell off his horse and tumbled to his

The Ancient Arms of

Menteith

death at Kinghorn in March 1286 the royal succession became hugely problematic. The last remaining heir, Alexander's grand-daughter, Margaret (known as the Maid of Norway), died on her way to Scotland in 1290 and Scotland entered a crisis period. The grasping and powerful King Edward I of England was asked to be the arbiter in the choice of a successor. There were fourteen competitors for the throne but the clear front runners were John Balliol and Robert Bruce.

Edward agreed to act as the arbiter but only if the candidates swore fealty to him, which they all subsequently did.

Walter Menteith had tied his loyalty firmly to the side of the Bruce faction. As early as 1286 the Earl was part of the Turnberry Band, an influential group who supported the claims of the Bruce family to the throne. John Balliol was the successful suitor to the throne but his Kingship was to last only four years when war with England and King Edward I ensued. On the outbreak of hostilities Walter's son, Earl Alexander, was actively supporting King John Balliol and the guardians of Scotland. In 1296 Alexander led a force which occupied Dunbar Castle but he was forced to surrender to the English and was then imprisoned in the Tower of London. He was released but gave up two sons as hostages for his good behaviour. This didn't prove terribly effective as his son Alan was at Robert Bruce's coronation at Scone in March 1306. Alan didn't live long to regret it as he was captured a short time later, possibly at the battle of Methven, and died in captivity.

Heroes and Villains 1: *John Menteith*

Scotland's greatest traitor?

*'When we consider the passionate devotion of the Scottish people to the memory of Wallace, there is scarcely room for wonder that the name of Menteith should have come down in the traditions of the country as that of **the greatest traitor in the national history**.'*[7]

Sir John Menteith was the second son of Earl Walter Stewart (Balloch). He was born sometime between 1260 and 1265 and

---

[7] Hutchison 1899 (italics by the author)

on reaching adulthood he was given the lands of Ruskie. His home was a castle built on an island, probably a crannog, in Loch Ruskie (now no longer visible).

He topped the catalogue of infamy when in August 1305 his men (no doubt locals) captured William Wallace at Robroyston and handed him over to Edward I of England. Needless to say, Sir John has not enjoyed the best press since that time but a more detailed look at the man and his actions paint a rather different picture.

Sir John, along with the Earls of Menteith, has as good a record as almost any noble family for backing the independence claims of Scotland against Edward I of England. He was an earlier supporter of Robert Bruce and was a signatory of the famous Turnberry Bond of 1286, which was in effect an agreement to support the Bruce claim to the throne. After John Balliol had become king and attempted to throw off the yoke of Edward, Sir John of Menteith was one of his supporters. In April, 1296, Edward of England invaded Scotland. Sir John, and of course his tenants, were in the Scottish army that was defeated at Dunbar. He was captured and imprisoned in England for over a year. He secured his freedom and the restoration of his lands of Ruskie by agreeing to serve King Edward in his French wars. On returning from France he soon resumed his activities against King Edward. In a communication to Edward, of October, 1301, he was designated 'The adversary of the King'. He continued in his opposition to the English occupation, and was, without doubt, well known to William Wallace.

By 1304 King Edward and his occupying army had virtual control of all of Scotland and with the exception of William Wallace, virtually all the ruling elite of Scotland (including John Comyn and Robert Bruce) had submitted to the English King. King Edward, wishing to test the loyalty of his new subjects, ordered them to become active in the search and apprehension of William Wallace. Sir John was one of these new subjects and he seems to have taken his new-found loyalty seriously. He quickly gained the trust of the English King, as in 1305 he was given the important custody of the castle, town, and Sheriffdom of Dumbarton. The circumstances by which he captured Wallace vary according to the sources. It is not certain who actually discovered the hiding-place of Wallace. One story tells of a servant, "Jack Short", being the traitor and acting on his information:

Menteith came and seized Wallace when he was still in bed.[8]

Sir John was rewarded for his actions[9] and for a short time was a loyal supporter of King Edward. He was chosen as a Scottish Commissioner and was one of the ten Scottish Representatives who met at the Westminster Parliament. He also continued in the office of Sheriff and keeper of the Castle of Dumbarton. In June 1306, King Edward conferred on him the Earldom of Lennox.

The impetus for Scottish independence seemed to have disappeared but the dramatic murder of John Comyn in Dumfries and the crowning of his assailant, Robert Bruce at Scone in March 1306 threw the nation into turmoil once again. By 1308 Robert Bruce's hold on Scotland was far from secure but despite this, Sir John went over to his side and once again became an enemy of King Edward (now the II) of England.

Perhaps the best way of reaching a judgement on Sir John was by examining the reaction of his contemporaries towards him at the time. King Robert Bruce seemed to hold no ill will. In 1308 Sir John was among those who acknowledged Bruce as their King in a letter 'of the nobles', sent to the King of France. He was with King Robert in the neighbourhood of Stirling in November 1313 and he along with his many tenants from our area almost certainly fought at Bannockburn (although there is no documentary evidence to that effect).

He may have accompanied Edward Bruce on his first expedition to Ireland in 1315 and accompanied by Sir Thomas Randolph in 1316, he definitely went to Ireland on a special mission. It is hoped that not too many of his tenants were with him on that terrible campaign.

Furthermore, Sir John was a signatory (as Guardian of the Earldom of Menteith) of the now very famous Declaration of Arbroath in

[8] Langtoft 8

[9] In a memorandum of the English Council mention is made of 40 marks "to be given to the valet who spied out William Waleys" and 60 marks to be divided among others who were present and "a hundred livres for John of Menteth".

1320, in which the signatories asserted the right of their country to independence and declared their determination to maintain it.

His final public act was in 1323 when he went to Newcastle and negotiated a truce for thirteen years with the English King. He died soon afterwards. Tradition avers that he died in his castle at Ruskie and was buried in the Priory of Inchmahome but no stone marks the place. At the time he was much mourned by his fellow country men but in later times that perception was to change dramatically. **Hero or Villain?** ... *you decide*

By 1323 Murdoch, the nephew of Sir John Menteith, had become Earl. He had sided with the English kings until 1317 but then went over to the Bruce camp. He is chiefly remembered today for being the man who informed King Robert of the Soules Conspiracy of 1320, when a group of dissatisfied nobles plotted to murder King Robert.

Murdoch was killed at the disastrous battle of Dupplin Moor in August 1332 when some of the disinherited Scottish exiled lords returned to attempt to regain their lands and put Edward Balliol on the Scottish throne. Murdoch is believed to have had a large contingent of local men amongst his followers and very many of them lost their lives in that calamitous battle.

The men of Menteith were to suffer again, as just fourteen years later they were to taste defeat once more, this time fighting for their new Earl, John Graham (*see* **Heroes and Villains 2**). It was probably of small consolation to them but Menteith got a new hero.

Heroes and Villains 2: *John Graham, Earl of Menteith*

John Graham had married Mary, daughter of Alan II, Earl of Menteith and then succeeded to the title. He accompanied David II in his invasion of England in 1346 and was present at the battle of Neville's Cross. By tradition he was by the King's side as the English archers began their deadly fusillade. He urged the King to send a body of cavalry to charge them in flank:

Give me but a hundred horse and I will engage to disperse them all; so shall we be able to fight more securely.

His appeal was turned down so he led his Menteith men in a charge anyway. His horse was killed under him and he was compelled to retreat. Ultimately the Earl was taken prisoner and along with King David he was imprisoned in the Tower of London. By the direct orders of the English King, Edward III, he was tried and condemned. His gruesome punishment, echoing that of William Wallace, was to be hanged, drawn, beheaded and quartered.

John Graham (*see* **Heroes and Villains 2**) was the first Graham landowner to appear in Menteith. His daughter, Margaret, was to make quite a splash in local circles, primarily as a result of her marital adventures. She was married four times and had five papal dispensations for the marriages (usually because of close family relationships). Firstly she married Lord Bothwell (the son of Andrew Murray and Christina Bruce) and thus helped to cement the Menteith family to the Bruce dynasty. On his death she married Thomas, Earl of Mar but they divorced soon after. The third marriage was to John Drummond in an attempt (unsuccessful) to settle the long running feud between the Menteiths and the Drummonds (*see page 26*). Her last marriage was to Robert Stewart, the Duke of Albany, son of Robert II and the builder of Doune Castle.

After Robert's death in 1420, his son Murdoch became Duke. James I, who had been in captivity in England, was released in 1424 and he considered that Robert and Murdoch had not made enough effort to secure his release from eighteen years of English captivity. As a result Murdoch was executed at Stirling Castle in 1425 and the Earldom of Menteith was then forfeited to the Crown, the king retaining the 'Stewartry of Menteith', which included the lands around the site of the future Thornhill. The western part of Menteith was granted to the Graham family who then took the title of 'Earl of Menteith'. Their involvement with the lands and people around the future Thornhill area was initially limited but when William, the third Earl of Menteith obtained the lands of Boquhapple in 1534 the Grahams were once more back on the local radar and destined to make a huge impact. (*see* **Heroes and Villains 3**).

The Drummonds

The Drummonds first appeared on the local scene around 1330 when the Earl of Menteith made over the lands of Boquhapple to Gilbert Drummond. Things didn't go well as the Drummonds were almost immediately drawn into a conflict with the Menteith family. The origin of the feud is now lost but it may have been to do with the neighbouring Earldom of Lennox where both families had large interests. Folklore also tells that the Drummonds attacked the Menteiths at the Tar of Ruskie and slew three of their chiefs:

> *urged by the desire to avenge the perfidy of Sir John Menteith on his descendants, and eager to exterminate the whole hated race*[10]

This tale is more likely a Victorian invention. The more probable origin is a boundary dispute with the Menteith Stewarts of neighbouring Ruskie soon after the Drummonds acquired Boquhapple. This tragically led to the murder of Bryce Drummond, the son of Gilbert Drummond and was quickly followed by a reprisal encounter at the Tar of Ruskie, where it appears that three of the Ruskie Menteith brothers, namely Walter, Malcolm and William, were killed.

The battlefield was probably near to the 'fort' at Tamnafalloch (*see page 5*). Further evidence of the conflict was discovered in the 19th century when several gravestones were found, one with the

---

[10] Hutchison, A.F., 1899

initial PS. Earlier still, in the 18th century a sword and coat of mail had been found on the same site.

King David II, in an effort to stop the blood feud, called a meeting between the principal feuding families on the 'banks of the river Forth'[11] on 17 May 1360. John Drummond, the leader of the Drummond family, met with John and Alexander Menteith and it appears that an agreement was reached and the parties agreed to stop all 'rancour and recrimination' against each other.

The Drummond family, although at that time the feudal vassals of the Earls of Menteith, went on to prosper and become the leading aristocratic family in the area. Possibly as a consequence of the ending of the feud the Drummonds acquired the barony of Kincardine around 1367 when John Drummond married Mary Muschet. John died before 1372 and his impressive tombstone can still be seen at Inchmahome Priory.

The Drummonds continued to expand their holdings to the east of present day Thornhill, primarily at the expense of the Muschet family. Blair Drummond was so named around 1684 and the Drummond Estates have formed a significant part of the local landscape right into recent times.

The Ancient Arms of

Muschet

The Muschets

The Muschets first arrived in Menteith in 1189 when Richard Montfiquet (to become Muschet) was granted the lands of 'Kincardin iuxta Strievelin' by William I. The Montfiquets came originally from Calvados in Normandy and arrived in England as a result of the Norman Conquest of 1066. In the 12th and early 13th centuries families of Norman origin were often invited into Scotland by the ruling monarchs, usually

---

[11] No precise location was given but it is likely to have occurred somewhere between Ruskie and Boquhapple, perhaps by the Forth to the south of Flanders Moss.

to act as strong–arm men to support the crown against the disorderly indigenous inhabitants, as seen to great effect in Galloway and Moray.[12] As incomers into a turbulent 'edge' region it is likely that the Muschets had a similar role and eventually they rose to high office being much favoured by the reigning monarchs. The Muschet castle of Kincardine, now long gone, was sited approximately where the parish church of Kincardine now stands. Their estate ultimately passed to the Drummond family around 1367 as a result of the marriage of Lady Mary Muschet to Sir John Drummond.

The fruits of this marriage were to have enormous implications for the future of Scotland. Their daughter was christened Anabella and she was to become Queen Anabella when she married Robert III (King of Scotland 1390–1406) with their youngest son becoming James I, King of Scotland. Therefore from the union of the Muschet and Drummond families we have the lineal descendants of all the royal house of Stuart, including Mary, Queen of Scots and Charles Edward Stuart (the so-called Bonnie Prince Charlie), much beloved of romantic literature.

Even though the bulk of their estates had passed to the Drummond family many Muschets remained in the areas of Burnbank and Craighead and were to continue to make their mark on history, alas often in a tragic way. A sad aspect of life at this time was the constant fear of the plague. There was no cure and it could strike without warning at any place and any time. In the old orchard of Kincardine Castle near Burnbank today can be seen a poignant memory to these terrible times.

A flat tombstone, and above it a more modern copy, records the death at 26 years old of Margaret Drummond. She was married to George Muschet and along with her three children tragically died near this spot on 10 August 1647. The plague had taken them all.

The inscription reads:

---

12 In Galloway the Fitz Allan (later to become Stewart) family and the Bruce families all received land on the marches of the unruly and independent minded Galwegians. Clan Fraser, Gordon and many more are of Norman origin.

A flat tombstone, and above it a more modern copy, records the death at 26 years old of Margaret Drummond, wife of George Muschet. Tragically, she and her three children died near this spot on 10 August 1647. The plague had taken them all.

Fig. 9 The Muschet plague grave

Here lyes the Corpse of Margaret Drummond, Frid Daughter to the Laird of Invermay, and Spouse to Sir George Muschet of Burnbanke, Her Age 26, Departit this Lyfe in the Wisitation with her Frie Children at Burnbanke, the 10th August, 1647

There is now little sign of the orchard in which this grave is said to be situated. The romantic story is that Margaret was buried here because she loved the area so much but the more prosaic truth is that this site was well enough away from the house to avoid the possibility of others being infected.

Burnbank has turned up other remarkable artefacts and as late as 2018 a green man was discovered. This was no Martian interloper but a carved key stone, probably the key stone of the archway leading into the Muschet home at Burnbank. It is believed to date from around 1598 (*see Fig. 1, page 1*).

Green man figures mainly date from the 11th to the 16th centuries but some pre-Christian sculpting has also been found. Quite what they represent remains an enigma but usually they are associated with concepts of fertility, rebirth or the annual cycle of growth.

A further gruesome reminder of these times occurred during road widening at the east end of Thornhill. It was said that the engineers found a number of skeletons when excavating the ground near to the present Lion and Unicorn. A likely explanation for these remains was that this was a grave for plague victims. Its position on the edge of Norriestoun would indicate the desire of the small settlement not to have the bodies buried within its boundary.

A more recent reminder of the danger of disease, this time cholera, is also associated with a Muschet. In the period of the early 19th century cholera was a constant scourge, especially where there was a problem with clean water. Although there was no apparent problem with clean water in the local area cholera made its appearance nonetheless. A visiting sheriff's officer of the name Muschet was sadly infected and did not make a recovery. He was buried in an isolated grave at the south eastern corner of the 'Upper Common' (probably the Skeoch) in order to be well away from the people of the village and their water supply and he lies there to this day.

The Craighead Muschets were still in possession of their lands in the 18th century and at least seven Muschets are recorded in the Craighead deeds between 1632 and 1732. Many other Muschets are also recorded in the local area including the family of Nicol Muschet of Boghall, who was to become infamous in his time (*see page 53*). By the late 17th century the Muschet family were noted for their devout adherence to the protestant cause and it is no surprise that one of their number, Lieutenant-Colonel Robert Muschet, fought with the Prince of Orange in 1681 and may have been involved with the campaigns against the deposed James VII in the north of Ireland. It is easy to imagine that relations with the fervent Jacobite, John Graham of nearby Boquhapple, would become severely strained.

The Grahams

The Graham connection with Menteith dates from 1425 when King James I granted the western portion of Menteith to the family. When William, the third Earl of Menteith, obtained the lands of Boquhapple in 1534 they would have received feudal superiority

1580, although the earliest written reference to Norrieston was
1649. The original Norrieston seems to have been centred to the
south of the present village, and present day 'Little Norrieston'
and Norrieston Farm mark the original sites. It was well posi-
tioned, being on a loop in the Cessintully Burn close to a direct
path between the Ford of Frew and the Ford of Lanrick by the
Teith and the Norries were to remain on this land for very many
years. Norrie's relatives and descendants became major local land-
holders. The large estate of nearby Boquhapple was in the hands
of Robert Norrie's son James by 1471. Furthermore, the husband
of an Elizabeth Norrie of Boquhapple was Walter Dog, who was
'camerarii de Menteith'[15] and the Keeper of Doune Castle. This is
the first mention of the 'Dog/Doig' family, a name still alive in Doig
Street in Thornhill.

The Dogs/Doigs

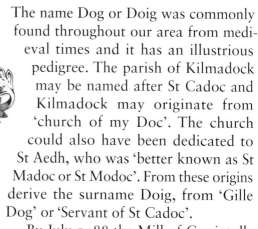

The Ancient Arms of

Doig

The name Dog or Doig was commonly
found throughout our area from medieval times and it has an illustrious
pedigree. The parish of Kilmadock
may be named after St Cadoc and
Kilmadock may originate from
'church of my Doc'. The church
could also have been dedicated to
St Aedh, who was 'better known as St
Madoc or St Modoc'. From these origins
derive the surname Doig, from 'Gille
Dog' or 'Servant of St Cadoc'.

By July 1488 the Mill of Cessintully
was in the possession of Walter Dog
and his mother and the Dogs/Doigs
soon began to widen their influence
by the acquisition of surrounding properties and estates. By July

---

[15] This is the Latin version of *chamberlain*, the definition of which is 'an officer
in charge of a noble, royal, or ecclesiastical household'. This hints at the local
importance of the Boquhapple estates.

1491 Walter, along with his brother James, had the lease of part of Coldoch Wester and in 1511 a John Doig controlled the estate of Gartincaber.[16]

Two generations later the Dogs came into conflict with the Muschet family. In 1564 another Walter, and his sons Alexander, John and Archibald were involved in a court case concerning the slaughter of Dionis Doge (*sic*). It appears that Dionis Doge, probably a son of Walter, was killed by John Muschet, John Morrison and James Morrison. To avoid a feud between the families a contract was drawn up which assigned damages. No more is heard of this conflict but the Dog family couldn't stay out of trouble. In 1575 the Dogs of this area were involved in a major altercation leading to the deaths of James Grahame of Bowquhoppill (*sic*), and Robert Norrie, son of James Norrie of Bowquhoppill (*sic*).

By 1605 the Dogs seem to have become reconciled to the Muschet family as a charter of that date is from William Muschet of Wester Spitteltoun (*sic*), whereby he sold to 'James Dog, the King's servant and Katherine Dow, his spouse, the twenty shilling land of old extent of Cessintullie (*sic*) otherwise called McCreistoun, in the lordship of Menteith'.

Later testimonies questioned Paul Doig, a tenant in Mossside of Kings Boquhapple, who had taken on farming duties from his father and he stated that the Dog family had farmed this area for many generations.

Ballangrew on the edge of Flanders Moss was also in the hands of the Dog/Doig family. Paul Doig of Ballangrew became yet another of that family to become embroiled in a little known conflict called Argyll's Rising or Argyll's Rebellion. In 1685 a group of Scottish Protestant exiles, led by Archibald Campbell, 9th Earl of Argyll, rose in support of the Monmouth Rebellion, aiming to overthrow the Catholic King James II and VII. Argyll's Rising was intended to tie down Royal forces in Scotland while Monmouth's army marched

---

16 An interesting side aspect to this family arises in the Royal Accounts of April 1497 where they note the sum 'giffen to Jame Dog to by fut ballis to the King,' (James IV). This is the earliest known reference to football. The earliest surviving football is from about 1540, discovered in 1981 in the roof of the Queen's Chamber, Stirling Castle. It is made from leather and a pig's bladder and is held by the Stirling Smith Art Gallery and Museum in Stirling.

on London. Argyll, the chief of Clan Campbell, had hoped to raise several thousand men amongst his followers and it was expected that many Presbyterians in southern Scotland would join them. An opposing Royalist force led by the Marquess of Atholl was raised and as part of this force Paul served with the Perthshire troop of horse commanded by Lord William Murray, under Cameron of Lochiel. They were camped near Inveraray when a contingent of Clan Cameron mistook them for Argyll's men and attacked them. Five local officers were killed including Paul Dog and a 'Napeir of Baluhapple' (*sic*). It is interesting that this local laird's support of the royalist cause preceded Graham of Boquhapple's adventures at the battle of Killiecrankie and indicated that the sympathies of many in the Thornhill area tended towards the Jacobite side.

The Napiers

Perhaps the family to have the greatest local influence were the Napiers. The dynasty that in 1696 were responsible for the estab-

Sans tache

Napier

lishment of Thornhill first appeared locally in a charter dated the 16 July 1462. Mary of Gueldres, the wife of King James II and then Regent following his death granted to John Napier the lands of Calziemuck in Ruskie. John soon began to style himself as John Napier of Ruskie, even though Ruskie seemed to be primarily his country retreat. He spent most of his time in Edinburgh where he became a bailie in 1463 and he later sat in the Scottish parliament. John cemented his local links when he married Elizabeth, one of the two daughters of Murdoch Menteith of Ruskie. He was later to lose his life at the battle of Sauchieburn in 1488.

The Napiers held the lands of Ruskie for a number of generations and by the mid-16th century Archibald Napier was head of the family. He was not without his troubles and like most of our local families he became embroiled in a number of disputes. One was apparently of long standing and occasionally had led to violence. This feud was between the Napier tenants at Calziemuck and the Grahams of Boquhapple and was based on disagreements concerning boundaries and commonality of land. In 1591 matters apparently came to a head as a result of the ploughing and sowing by Napier's tenants of land which the surrounding feuars alleged to be commonalty; similar flare-ups between the same parties were to be repeated in 1611, 1612, and 1613. By this time Archibald's son, John, born in 1550 when Archibald was only 17, was the Laird who had to sort out the problem.

John maybe had other things on his mind. Although today digital calculating devices have made the discovery and use of Logarithms and 'Napier's bones' (an early calculating methodology) obsolete and almost forgotten, they have been of immense importance in the development of mathematics. By his inventions the most complicated problems in astronomy, navigation, and other sciences could be solved by a relatively easy and certain method. The Dictionary of National Biography notes:

> *The invention necessarily gave a great impulse to all the sciences which depend for their progress on exact computation. Napier's place among great originators in mathematics is fully acknowledged* [17]

If mathematics, physics, astronomy and near neighbours were not enough to worry about, the Napier lands were also regularly plagued by raids from the Highland clans of the north. Exhibiting the tendency for the local area to suffer from the 'borderland syndrome', John attempted to bring peace to his land and his tenants. He entered into a mutual bond with Campbell of Lawers in 1611 undertaking:

> *to bring to punishment any MacGregors or other Highland broken men who should trouble Napier's lands in Lennox or*

---

[17] *Dictionary of National Biography, 1885–1900*, Volume 40. Napier, John by William Rae MacDonald

Menteith, the latter to assist Lawers and his family in all their lawful and honest affairs

John did appear to sort out his boundary issues, even obtaining a disposition of the lands of Boquhapple in favour of himself and his son Robert in June 1616 and finally, only months before his death in April 1617, he purchased from an Archibald Edmonstone 'his twenty merk lands of (King's) Boquhapple with the pertinents in the Stewartry of Menteith and Sheriffdom of Perth.'

The Napiers were often absentee landlords from their estates at Ruskie and Boquhapple but not by choice. They had become increasingly involved in the affairs of the state. James' son Archibald

Fig. 10 Ballinton (Napier coat of arms)

This marriage bas relief of c. 1619 shows the Napier coat of arms above a lintel. The initials A. N. are believed to represent Archibald Napier and M.G. Margaret Graham. This marriage united the two leading families of the area and helped to bring about an end to a long existing feud.

became as well-known as his celebrated father in his day. Amongst many other honours he became the Treasurer Depute of Scotland, was created a Baronet of Nova Scotia and in May 1627 was raised to the Peerage of Scotland as a Lord of Parliament, with the title Lord Napier of Merchistoune.

In 1640 Scotland entered a period of crisis and battle lines were drawn. The Civil War had broken out and Archibald declared himself as a loyal supporter of King Charles I. He was imprisoned by the Covenanters along with his son, also Archibald, but his son escaped. Lord Napier and his family were then imprisoned in Edinburgh Castle and fined £10,000. They were transferred to Linlithgow but son Archibald managed to organise their escape. Both Lord Napier and his son then joined the famous Marquis of Montrose (Lord Napier's brother-in-law) and fought with him at the Battle of Philiphaugh (Lord Napier was then over 70 years of age). Alas for Archibald the battle became a rout but he and his son managed to escape unharmed. He died in 1645 but son Archibald had gone into exile overseas and was never to return to Scotland.

Even though Archibald was ultimately pardoned, his finances and those of the Napier family, were in ruins. He was forced to mortgage his lands of Merchiston and his lands in the west (presumably including Boquhapple and Ruskie) were 'ruined and overburdened'. Archibald died in 1660 just before his uncle, James Graham, the Marquis of Montrose, was executed in Edinburgh for his support of King Charles.

Montrose had been excommunicated and was originally buried in unconsecrated ground but son Archibald's widow, Elizabeth, sent men by night to remove his heart. This relic she placed in a steel case made from his sword and placed the whole in a gold filigree box. The heart in its case was proudly kept by the Napier family for several generations but was sadly lost during the French Revolution.

It is ironic that the Napiers had become related to their former antagonists the Grahams through the Montrose marriages and their support of the Stuart kings. The Napiers were ruined by their support of the Marquis of Montrose during the Civil War and the Grahams were to suffer equally from their support of kinsman John Graham of Claverhouse just 30 years later (*see page 39*).

Thus in the early 1660s the lands of Ruskie and Boquhapple passed to another Archibald Napier. This Archibald was a great-grandson of John Napier and was descended through Robert Napier, the second son of John's second marriage, and then from Robert's eldest son, Archibald. He married Annabel Linton in 1679 and made the family home at Ballinton. Above the lintel at Ballinton can be seen the coats of arms of the Napier and Graham families. The initials A.N. are believed to represent Archibald Napier.

Archibald had a tough job in attempting to reverse the fortunes of the lands he had just inherited. Just a few years earlier Archibald Napier had described the lands as 'ruined and overburdened'. It cannot have helped his state of mind when in 1685 his brother was killed by the Camerons in the same pro-government action against the Earl of Argyll in which Paul Dog also lost his life.

In 1688 the Stuart King James II and VII was ousted, to be replaced by the joint monarchy of the Protestants William and Mary from the Netherlands. Although John Napier had been a stalwart protestant, later Napiers, despite remaining protestant, had shown a predisposition to support the Stuart family. In addition Archibald's brother had been killed in just such a service.

Following the 'glorious revolution' of 1688, as it later became known, parts of Scotland, especially the Highlands, were in open revolt and the battle of Killiecrankie was to take place less than one year later.

Graham of Boquhapple, no doubt accompanied by a significant number of his tenants, played a prominent part in this rising. Major William Graham of Boquhapple was a first cousin of John Graham of Claverhouse, the 1st Viscount Dundee. Claverhouse in Scottish history is both revered and reviled in equal measure. He earned the (rather unfair) sobriquet 'Bluidy Clavers' for his actions against the Covenanters in south west Scotland but conversely he became a Jacobite hero as 'Bonnie Dundee'. After the Revolution of 1688 William of Orange and his wife Mary became joint English and Scottish sovereigns but Claverhouse remained loyal to King James VII of Scotland. He famously rallied the Scottish clans loyal to the Jacobite cause, including the Graham family, and won a stunning victory at Killiecrankie in July 1689. By his side throughout the campaign was William Graham of Boquhapple.

Heroes and Villains 3: *Major William Graham of Boquhapple*

Wilhelm Graham of Boquhapple, the first cousin of John
Graham of Claverhouse, the 1st Viscount Dundee, had
become an officer in Claverhouse's Cavalry in 1682 and was
involved in the campaigns in 1683 and 1684 against Covenanters
in Dumfries and Galloway. He was very close to Claverhouse,
being godfather to Claverhouse's son. He, along with a significant
number of his tenants from the Boquhapple area, was by his side
throughout the Killiecrankie campaign. Claverhouse lost his life at
Killiecrankie and the uprising ultimately failed but William Graham
survived and (in his absence) faced the charge of treason against
the state.

Treason

*... the deceased John, Viscount of Dundee and Major William
Graham of Boquhapple ... (the 3rd name cited amongst the other
20 leaders named) ... they did rise and continue in open arms
against their majesties' authority and government ... of the month
of April 1689 ... did attack a certain number of their majesties'
forces ... the other persons above-named, having raised and
assembled several thousands of rebels and Highland robbers ...
oppressing and destroying their majesties' good and loyal subjects
and to oppose their forces. And upon 26 July 1689 ... did in a
plain battle attack their majesties' army between the Blair of Atholl
and the pass of Killiecrankie, and did kill and wound several of
their majesties' forces and good subjects. And thereafter ... the
other persons aforesaid and their accomplices did attack their
majesties' forces at Dunkeld where they did kill Lieutenant
Colonel William Clelland ... and several others of their majesties'
officers and faithful soldiers ... and sent out parties to murder
and destroy their majesties' good subjects and to rob and plunder
them of their goods. And the particular acts of rebellion, treason,
rising and continuing in arms against their majesties' authority
and government, the assaulting of their forces, the garrisoning of
houses and strengths, the harbouring, corresponding with open
rebels and traitors, and the falling upon, wounding or robbing their*

*majesties' forces, and the other crimes above-mentioned, were
committed by the persons above-named ...*

*And the king and queen's majesties and the estates of parliament,
having considered the aforesaid libel and indictment for high
treason ... against the forenamed persons, defenders, with the
depositions of the witnesses who were cited ... they hereby find
the aforesaid crime of treason ... (that the forenamed persons were
actually in arms against their majesties after the 4 May 1689)...
sufficiently verified and proven against the said John, Viscount of
Dundee ... Major William Graham of Boquhapple... their majesties
and the estates of parliament ... decree and adjudge the said ...
Major William Graham ... and others...to be executed to the death,
demeaned as traitors and to underlie the pains of treason whenever
they shall be apprehended ... and ordain the said persons, their
name, fame, memory and honours to be extinct, their blood to
be tainted and their arms to be riven forth and deleted out of
the books of arms so that their posterity may never have place
nor be able hereafter to hold or enjoy any honours, offices, titles
or dignities in time coming. And the said persons immediately
above-named to have forfeited and lost all and sundry their lands,
heritages, tacks, steadings, rooms, possessions, goods and gear,
moveable and immoveable, whatsoever pertaining to them ...*[18]

Despite his outlaw status William managed to evade the hangman's
noose and fled to France, joining the exiled King James' court.
William did eventually return to Scotland at some stage (although
probably not to Boquhapple and Thornhill), as the next time we
hear of him he had been promoted to Colonel. He died intestate in
the Citadel of Leith in February 1736.

In view of the Napier families' recent history Archibald had to
show a balanced stance and he seemed to have the support of the
new Scottish Williamite administration. On the 24 May 1689, just

---

[18] *The Records of the Parliaments of Scotland to 1707*, K.M. Brown et al eds.
(St Andrews, 2007–18), (William II and Mary II: Translation, 1690, 15 April,
Edinburgh).

two months before the battle of Killiecrankie, the Scots Parliament issued a commission to him:

> *considering how necessary it is for their majesty's service and for the security of the country of Monteith … that the fords and ferries of the said river above Stirling be guarded and secured … therefore the estates reposing special trust and confidence in the loyalty, fidelity and good conduct of the persons after-named, do grant full power, warrant and commission to Archibald Napier of Boquhapple and James Stewart, younger of Ardvorlich, to raise and convocate in arms the number of 300 men or more, of their own and such other gentlemen and others of their neighbourhood on both sides of the said river of Forth, who are well affected to the present government, and may be willing to join and concur with them in the said service … with power to them to model the said 300 or more men into companies or a regiment … or with such numbers of them as shall be thought sufficient to guard and secure the said fords upon the river of Forth above Stirling, that none be allowed to pass the said fords and ferries, but such as are known to be well affected to the government, or have passes from the magistrates or commanding officers where they dwell, and to seize upon and secure all persons who are liable to the suspicion of being disaffected, or in opposition to the government, as also to guard and secure the said country and bounds from thefts, robberies, degradations, oppressions and others violences to be committed upon any of their majesties' peaceable subjects …* [19]

By 1695 the risings had failed, William Graham and his Boquhapple tenants were either out of the country or quietened, the country was at peace and Archibald Napier could turn his mind to other matters.

---

[19] http://www.rps.ac.uk. *William II and Mary II: 14 March, Edinburgh*, Convention, Parliamentary Register, Edinburgh 24 May 1689.

4

Rob Roy and the Clan Wars

THE ACTIVITIES OF THE LEADING FAMILIES OFTEN revolved around the relationships between the lowland areas to the south and the nearby clans to the north. There was no sharp divide locally as common cultural connections were the norm. Indeed, three names in the initial feuing lists (McLaren, McCulloch and McKean) were all of Gaelic origin with families originally coming from Highland Menteith and Strathearn. It was commonplace for the families such as the Napiers and Grahams to work in close association with Highlanders and their clans. Nevertheless, some strains did begin to show, especially with regard to the Clan Gregor. The MacGregors, following a number of disagreements with the crown, tended to operate in a semi-lawless capacity. It was not uncommon for their raiding parties to descend upon the more fertile carse lands and the lands of Lennox to the west in search of cattle, or to offer 'protection' with the infamous 'mall dubh', or blackmail as it has become in English. We have few specific records of raids in Thornhill or the Norrieston area but nearby areas such as Kippen and Gartmore habitually suffered. An inquiry held at Holyrood in 1585 had the following subject matter:

> *For samekle as his king's majesty and the Lords of his Pryvy Council are creditably informed that his good and peaceable subjects inhabiting the country of the Lennox, Menteith, Struilingschyre, and Stratherne are heavily opressed by reif, stouth, sorning and other crimes dayly and nightly used upon them by certain theives, lymmers, and sorners lately broke loose upon them furth of the braes of the countries next adjacent*

One local example was related by Ramsay of Ochtertyre. Robert Buchanan of Moss-side described to him how, in about 1640, his grandfather's house was plundered by MacGregors and he was taken prisoner and hidden on a hillside above Callander. Lord

George Drummond raised a posse of local men and set out to rescue him. The rescue was apparently successful and without further incident but serves to demonstrate how in some aspects the local area must have been very like the frontier towns of the USA west.

The frequent passage of clansmen through the area to the lowlands and to the market at Doune may have been a continuing source of tension to the now predominantly Scots-speaking community. The local records give reminders of the days of Rob Roy Campbell MacGregor. As a leading member of the infamous 'Lennox Horse' he offered the dubious privilege of offering protection against cattle reivers. He himself was no mean cattle reiver as exemplified in the famous 'hership' of Kippen. In 1691, Rob Roy and his men captured 200 head of cattle and attacked Kippen in passing, adding all its cattle to their haul. However, as they were fording the Forth at Frew a detachment of dragoons surprised them. Although battle was joined the highly trained dragoons were routed by the Highland men. Rob Roy would have cause to remember the Frew area a few years later following his altercation with the Duke of Montrose over the loss of £1000 Scots by his chief drover. Rob Roy, in great debt, had lost his land and holdings and was outlawed. He was finally captured somewhere in the local area and was tied up and taken towards Stirling via the Frews. Somehow he managed to cut his ropes and he leapt off his horse, escaping into the Forth at Frew and so making one of his most famous escapes.

In 1750 the wild streak in the Macgregor family came back to the surface when Rob Roy's son, Robin Oig MacGregor, accompanied by his brother and others, rushed into a house at Edinbilly, Balfron and presented guns, swords and pistols to the terrified family. They then tore a 20 year old girl, Jean Kay, from her mother's arms and bore her off despite her screams and protestations. Afterwards a forced marriage took place at Rowardennan. The country was outraged and finally Robin was apprehended near Gartmore and taken to Edinburgh for trial. James Fairfoul of Braendam was one of the Justices of the Peace who were prominent in the proceedings against him and helped to bring about a conviction. Robin's first wife, by then deceased, was a Graham from Wester Boquhapple, a near neighbour to Braendam. Robin Oig was hanged in Edinburgh on 1 February 1754.

Part Two

Thornhill On The Map

The Growth of a Village 1696–1914

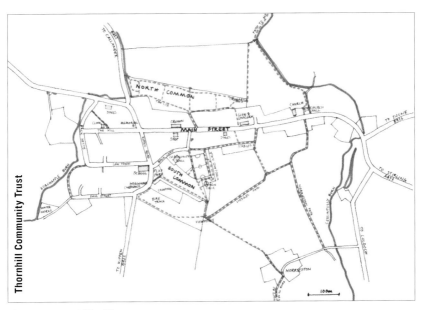

Thornhill Community Trust

Fig. 11 Thornhill village map

5

1696: Thornhill on the Map

IN 1995 RESEARCH BY GEORGE DIXON IN the Central Region Archives led to the discovery of an inventory of the earliest feu charters of the village of Thornhill. Thus began the process which led the community to celebrate the tercentenary of the birth of the village in 1996.

Immediately to the east of Archibald Napier's Boquhapple lands lay the hamlet of Norriestoun. Although it was by then the ecclesiastical centre for the western section of Kincardine it had no economic or trading function, so in 1695 Archibald turned to the Scottish Parliament for some assistance. In fact, in 1695 the Parliament were to authorise the holding of 18 weekly markets, 3 annual markets and 85 annual fairs in 40 different locations throughout Scotland. Archibald ensured that his estate became one of them:

That in all time coming here be four fayrs settled and established yearly at the Toun of King's Balquhaple in the parochin of Kincardine

He also obtained permission to have a weekly market on Thursday with four larger fairs to take place on 20 October (Margaret's), 14 November (Martinmass), 1st Tuesday in March (Lenton) and 2nd Tuesday in June (Hill's) each year, each one to last 8 days. Along with this huge trade boost he also received the right to exact 'toll and custom'. All he now needed were some people to make his markets and fairs a financial success.

The markets began operating in 1696 and by 10 February of the same year he began to tackle his people problem by granting feus of land on a gently rising thorn-covered ridge which ran westwards from his eastern boundary with Norrieston.

His plan, whilst visionary, was not unique. In Scotland there were 22 planned new settlements between the 1670s and the early 1700s including nearby Buchlyvie, established in 1672. Indeed, perhaps this may have been the nearby catalyst which prompted Archibald to begin his new venture.

Initially the feuing and building was on a small scale. The feus were of a standard size of 21 ells (65 feet) wide by 66 ells (203 feet) long or ratios of this size, and originally were fronting the new 'High Street', not as today called Main Street because it was not the main road of the time. The existing 'main' route (because it would hardly warrant the term road) ran to the north of the present Main Street, linking up the corner of the church land at Norrieston with the Aberfoyle Road and following the approximate line of the present path through the North Common.

The feuing, despite very limited marketing opportunities, was an immediate success and the attractions of the site along with the freedom inherent in the feu rights on offer were enough to attract 15 new settlers on the founding day of 10 February 1696.

It is interesting to speculate on Archibald's motives for feuing this ground. Almost certainly he needed the income. The Napier support of the monarchy during the calamity of the Civil War had brought the family almost to complete ruin and it is likely that Archibald was still picking up the pieces. His role during the more recent Killiecrankie crisis (*see page 39*) hardly helped his cause either as the maintenance of his small army must have been vastly expensive. Furthermore there was not a lot of money around anyway. The area was experiencing a long period of appalling weather which became known as the 'little ice age'. This had led to a series of nationally catastrophic harvest failures which affected almost all parts of Scotland for a number of years from 1695. Poverty was very much in evidence and it is unlikely that Napier's tenants would have been spared the general hardships found throughout the land.

No more than wild speculation but maybe even investment in the Darien scheme played a part. This was the ill-fated attempt by the Scottish parliament to found a colony at Darien, near the site of the present day Panama Canal. The capital needed for this endeavour was enormous and there was a huge patriotic movement in Scotland to support the venture. In the process it came close to bankrupting the country when the speculation failed. Three Napiers contributed funds. Archibald was not mentioned by name but may well have been involved with other family members in a consortium.

Whatever his motives, the scheme went ahead and in 1696 Archibald Napier can justly claim to have established the village of Thornhill. The layout of houses and gardens on the Main Street of Thornhill today is remarkably similar to that established by the first feuing process. The village was to have a strong linear form with roadside cottages lining the High Street fronting extended garden feus, all enclosed by village common land.

It is interesting to attempt to identify the first feus from their present geographical setting. Dixon arrived at a feuing plan based on the premise that the present 'cross lanes' at 50 and 47 Main Street seen today held a similar position in 1696, thus giving a recognisable point to begin placing the feus as entered in the register of Sasines:

the wynd lyeing South and Northward throwgh the toune of Thornehill

It is unclear whether these wynds are in exactly the same position today as they were in 1696, especially the Loan on the north side leading to the North Common, now called Gray's Loan, but it is a very useful starting point. Initial feus were taken from these central points to the base of the ridge to the east, and from these we can discover the 'pilgrim fathers' of Thornhill.

James Spittal and his wife Agnes McKean took up a large feu at the base of the ridge towards the march with Norrieston, probably on the site of the current Lion and Unicorn Hotel. This plot contained several other existing buildings. The rest followed the more direct feuing plan. The other first day feus included:

On the south side from the Loan 'cross wynd' eastwards to the Spittal feu:

James Law (Kings Boquhapple)

John Spittal (Kings Boquhapple) shoemaker

Donald McLaren (Kings Boquhapple) weaver

Duncan Smith (Bridgend of Doune)

Robert Sands (Cardross)

John Maxwell (Murdieston) Notary

Robert Paterson (Burnside)

James McCulloch (Murdieston)

Andrew Chalmers (Mill of Cessintully)

Immediately west of the Loan:

John Mitchell (Wester Boquhapple)

On the north side running eastwards from the 'cross wynd':

Thomas Paterson (McOrriston)
William Paterson (Boghall)
William Mitchell (Kings Boquhapple)
Andrew Mitchell (Kings Boquhapple)

Only five more feus were granted over the next three years. Later in 1696 were two to John McCulloch west of the cross wynd on the north side and in 1699 one each to Archibald McCulloch and Alexander Fletcher, both edging the village westwards further up the ridge.

David Turner also took a feu perhaps much further westwards in a spot:

commonly called Back o' the hill

Following the initial enthusiasm the village was not to grow significantly larger for many years, primarily as a result of the very difficult economic circumstances operating in the country as a whole. Several successive harvests had failed in the late 1690s and Scotland reported great loss of life.

the harvest became altogether disastrous, first by great winds and thereafter by rains, yea and storms of snow &c. ... the plague of famine ... occasioned so great a mortality ... that the year ... [1700] ... so was most calamitous ... multitudes died for want of bread ... People die[d] in the streets and high wayes in great numbers ... in some paroches at least the one half died for want [20]

All the initial feuars were local men, most from within a mile of the new village and this illustrates that prior to the establishment of the village there was already considerable local settlement in the existing fermtouns. Hearth taxes (levied in 1694 for hearths in

---

[20] Dixon, 1995, quoting A.P.S., vol. XI (1824), pp. 163–7.

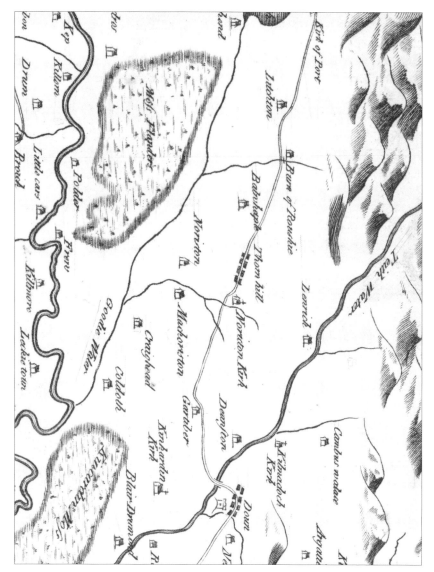

Fig. 12 Edgar's survey map 1746

One of the first available maps. It is not strictly accurate but gives a good impression of the area at this early date. Thornhill and Norrieston are shown but both appear to be very small. The main surrounding houses such as Lanrick, Gartiber (Gartincaber) and Coldoch are shown. Note the very large extent of the Kincardine Moss and Flanders Moss. Thornhill would have been a very remote community at this time.

permanent dwellings) showed that Boquhapple (Kings), Boquhapple (western) and Norrieston each had nine permanent dwelling houses, often accommodating multiple tenancies.

Which is the oldest house in Thornhill? The Lion and Unicorn Hotel by repute dates from 1635 and therefore pre-dates the formation of Thornhill itself and indeed could therefore claim to be one of the oldest inns in Scotland. This is not impossible as coaching inns tended to be spaced regularly to enable changes of horses to be made and there was an early need for such an inn near this site as the military road from Blair Drummond to Inversnaid was developed. The present building would probably be on the site of James Spittal's feu of 1696. It is not recorded as such although it is recognised that buildings did pre-exist here.

Fig. 13 Sorley's Inn, the present-day Lion and Unicorn

It is claimed that the Lion and Unicorn on the right of the photograph is the oldest building in Thornhill. Although known as the Commercial Hotel until relatively recently it shows the wall plaques of the Lion and Unicorn (its present name) high up on the wall. This may indicate an earlier name celebrating the Act of Union between England and Scotland. Another possible explanation of the plaques is also political, as the symbols would represent support for the Hanoverian kings during the Jacobite disturbances 1688–1746. 'Commercial' was a popular inn name after the coming of the railways in the mid-19th century.

It is difficult to date with substantiated proof the oldest house in the village. The central and eastern portion of Main Street appears to have the oldest pedigree but there were isolated scattered settlements to both west and east. 2 Low Town is said to date from 1701. Hillview also lays claim to be an early feu and its position at the 'top' of the village would give some geographical credence to the claim, despite doubt about village expansion as far as The Hill until the second half of the 18th century. There are a number of other houses of 18th century origin on the Main Street and The Hill and they may also have claims. Springfield, on the Callander road, once lay astride the old through-road to the north of the village and by repute was a Drovers Inn in the 18th century.

The oldest house in Norrieston still in present day use appears to be Norrieston House and the adjoining Heatherlea, situated across the road from the Church. Its position in Norrieston, by the site of the old Chapel of Ease, would agree with an early origin, and the deeds of the present day house show that ownership was transferred from James Montgomerie to John Steuart (a common early spelling) in 1757. The house construction was almost certainly earlier than this date. Knowehead, the house once known as 'Pipers Cottage' at the eastern entrance to the village, also pre-dates 1745, as probably does Little Norrieston. The Mill of Cessintully will pre-date them all, although its position lies just outside of the village boundary and little now remains of the original buildings. Overall, the Thornhill record seems to lie with 61 Main Street, for which deeds are still extant giving a date of 1749. Further searches through the sasine registers may clarify this position.

6

Murder Most Extraordinary

JUST SIX YEARS AFTER THE BATTLE OF Sherrifmuir Nicol Muschet of Boghall, one of the few remaining local members of that ancient Kincardine family, was executed in the Grassmarket of Edinburgh for the murder of his young wife, Margaret. This murder was to scandalise not just the people of Thornhill but the whole nation, as it was fully documented and sensationalised through cheap available chapbooks, the equivalent of today's tabloid press. However, in their favour, they did allow us to read the thoughts of the assailant, his mother and his accomplices; words which spring off the page after almost 300 years.

Nicol was born in 1695 at Boghall, just to the east of Thornhill and would have watched the young village grow and develop as he grew to adulthood. His parents were described as 'eminent where they lived for piety' and he was brought up as a strict Presbyterian, as could only have been expected amongst the fervent local covenanting Muschets. He attended the Edinburgh Medical College and in 1716 became a surgeon's apprentice. For reasons unknown he soon left his new profession to return to Boghall. Maybe Boghall did not meet his aspirations as after a short period he returned to Edinburgh. It was then that he met a young lady named Margaret Hall. Nicol described Margaret as a "girl of highly dubious virtue". Despite this (or more probably because of this, as the rumour was that she had fallen pregnant) Nicol and Margaret got married after only a few weeks together. Nicol insisted that although he found her company "repellent" Margaret's "shameful pursuit of him" led to their marriage. Unsurprisingly the marriage soon failed and Nicol looked for ways to extricate himself from the matrimonial arrangements without penalty, financial or otherwise.

At this stage Nicol discussed his problem with James Campbell of Burnbank, likely a boyhood friend (presumably this is the Burnbank situated little more than a mile from Boghall) and James[21]

---

21 James Campbell was described by Nicol as 'the Vice-Regent of the Devil'.

offered a possible solution. In exchange for a fee, he would help Muschet obtain a divorce by acquiring legal affidavits from witnesses testifying to "the whorish practices of Margaret Hall." One plan consisted of taking Margaret to the home of a friend (a town Magistrate) drug her with laudanum and while she was unconscious bring in another friend — "a Professor of Languages", who would then ravish her and tell all of the sordid behaviour of Margaret. This plan was never brought to fruition because a lawyer, James Russell, informed them that unless they could prove prior acquaintance between Hall and the unnamed Professor, this evidence of her "infidelity" would not be admissible.

This setback was far from the end of the story. Relatives of Nicol, James Muschet and his wife Grissel, then joined the plot and for a fee they also agreed to help him.

Continuing the schemes to prove that Margaret was a loose woman proved to be ineffective and expensive so Nicol Muschet, now becoming increasingly desperate, decided that murder was the only option. Firstly, James Campbell suggested poison and James Muschet gave Margaret 'a dram liberally laced with mercury' but although she became sick she soon recovered. Over a short period of time several more doses of mercury were administered to her but Margaret was made of stern stuff and refused to die.

The next plan was very simple. James Muschet would get Margaret drunk and then drown her in a pond. An alternative proposition from Grissel suggested that her husband would "on a pretence of kindness" take Margaret out riding with him and when they came to a river he would hurl her into the water. Campbell countered this by suggesting James should simply knock Margaret on the head and throw her "into some Hole without the Town, and immediately thereafter flee to Paris", but James declined. By May 1720 another plan had been formulated. Grissel would invite Margaret to her lodgings and keep her there until a late hour. When Margaret was walking home her husband, lying in wait, would batter her to death. They attempted to put this into practice several times but on each occasion it was aborted because "somebody going up or down prevented it."

Had the end result not been so tragic this farcical situation would have been highly comedic and Nicol was close to abandoning his plans to bring about the murder of his seemingly invulnerable spouse. Grissel Muschet was more uncompromising:

Is it reasonable, think you, so to do, when my husband and I have wasted so much time and pains to accomplish that design, and in expectation of our reward, now to give it over?

So, the murder attempts continued to be made but with no more success. By October 17 1720 Nicol Muschet realised that his expensively hired assassins were not very good at their job and so decided to do it himself. He borrowed a knife from his landlady and invited his wife to take a walk with him. He led her into King's Park near the palace of Holyrood and then launched a frenzied attack. Margaret put up a huge struggle but ultimately it was to no avail.

Nicol Muschet then left the lifeless Margaret and returned home, boasting of his "horrid wickedness" to his landlady and to the Muschets. At the time of her death Margaret was just sixteen years old.

Grissel and her husband assured Nicol that all would be fine because they would perjure themselves in his defence. Predictably, their very next step was to tell law enforcement officers everything they knew about the murder, with Grissel even leading the City Guard to Nicol's lodgings. Nicol quickly admitted the act and signed a confession. That November a letter to Nicol (then imprisoned in the Edinburgh Tollbooth) which purported to be from Nicol's mother, Jean, 'Lady Boghall', was published. Religious fervour was not unusual in Scotland at this time but nonetheless this was an extraordinary letter from a mother to her son, It was, of course, everyone else's fault (and this included the devil himself) as she spoke of his falling into sin and urging him to confess and repent for his crimes to obtain divine forgiveness:

I cannot now in writing give you such Expressions of Affection, as I formerly used, for you have by your Wicked and Abominable Crimes, made me ashamed and sorry to own the Relation of a Mother to you.
Woe is me that ever I should have born and Nursed up such a Rebellious Son ... but ...(he) has now added ... Grievous and Horrid Sin to all former debaucheries ... Enormously

shewing that thy only Pleasure and Delight was in doing the
Works of the Devil, and Reproaching thy Maker, by Sinning
presumptuously against him.
... see that you Spend, what ... time now Remains,
in a Solemn, Serious, Preparation for Death [22]

While imprisoned Nicol produced his full confession and dying speech, in which he "forgave Campbell, the Muschets and others", although he described them as being entirely responsible for his deeds.

Nicol Muschet was hanged on January 6 1721 in Edinburgh's Grassmarket.

The story did not end there. James and Grissel Muschet once again turned King's Evidence leading to James Campbell facing charges. He was found guilty for being 'art and part' in the numerous attempts to murder Margaret Hall and he was sentenced to transportation to the West Indies for life. Numerous pamphlets were published on the murder, as well as the letter from Nicol's mother to Nicol whilst he was imprisoned. They including Nicol Muschet's 'dying speech' which became a 52-page pamphlet [23], a poem purporting to be from James Campbell of Burnbank and an elegy, which became a 'best-seller', printed shortly after the murder (*see Appendix 8*). [24] In addition a cairn was erected over the site of Margaret's death in King's Park, although the monument has been relocated over the centuries. 'Muschet's Cairn' also featured in Sir Walter Scott's novel *The Heart of Midlothian.*

---

[22] This section is a much abridged version from the Broadside showing the full letter of Lady Boghall to Nicol Muschet. The full version is available online (*see* bibliography).

[23] Muschet Nicol, *The Confession, &c., of Nicol Muschet of Boghall*, 1818.

[24] *Elegy, on the deplorable Death of Margaret Hall, barbarously murder'd by her Husband Nicol Mushet of Boghall, Monday Night the 17 October 1720, in the 17th Year of her Age.* https://digital.nls.uk/broadsides/view/?id=15621.

7

Ye Jacobites by Name

THE INVOLVEMENT OF THE GRAHAMS OF BOQUHAPPLE in the Killiecrankie rising would have inevitably involved a large number of local tenants and their memories would be vivid. Therefore, not surprisingly, the major local landowners were cautious about becoming too involved in further risings. Thus the Jacobite risings of 1708 and 1715 had a relatively minor impact on the village. Nevertheless, locals held their breath when the large Jacobite army of the Earl of Mar camped at Kinbuck near Dunblane on the eve of the Battle of Sherrifmuir in 1715. They would have watched some of the MacGregor contingent under our old acquaintance, Rob Roy, rushing along the military road towards the battle area. Indeed, many of these participants would have been well known to them from when they visited the new Thornhill fairs with their cattle. The MacGregors paused along their route to capture 20 government guns in and around Callander but stood on the sidelines when the Sherrifmuir engagement took place. There is no evidence of local connections to this rebellion although it is highly likely that there were mixed feelings about support and involvement.

The Jacobite rising of 1745 is better documented. Although the army of Charles Edward Stuart rarely rose above 5000 men it has imposed a rich picture upon our history. In 1746 there were 490 men aged 14–60 in the parish of Kincardine and of them 10 local men were engaged with the Jacobite army and were almost certainly present at the ill-fated battle of Culloden. This number is surprisingly small because most of the Drummond family, feudal superiors for much of the village, were heavily engaged with the Prince and James Drummond, the Earl of Perth, was the joint leader of the Jacobite forces. In addition the Haldanes of Lanrick were also active and devoted to the Jacobite cause. However, in view of the disastrous impact of supporting the Stuart monarchy on the Napiers, the Grahams and the Doigs it is not surprising that most villagers preferred to remain on the sidelines.

The Thornhill volunteers would probably have signed up when the Jacobite Army moved through the area on the 12 September 1745, prior to crossing the Forth at Frew in an attempt to miss the heavily fortified bridge and castle of Stirling. They were expecting to be attacked at the crossing by Gardiner's Dragoons, but the dragoons fled back to Stirling at the first sight of the Jacobites. Local tradition tells that Prince Charles spent that night in a house where presently stands Mossside of Boquhapple. Unfortunately this is not the case, as he slept in the house of MacGregor of Balhaldie in Dunblane but the confusion may have occurred because the grandfather of Mr Syme of Moss-side did receive a sword from Charles Edward Stuart for the loan of a horse on that day.

It is certain that Charles' advance guard of officers and clansmen were billeted in the main houses in the village and wined and dined at the local hostelries. The advance guard included Duncan McPharrie McGregor, who commanded a company of the Highland army and slept this night in Thornhill. Mr Ballantyne, who lived in 'Piper's Cottage' at the time recorded that the army commandeered a horse from him. The horse was obviously not a Jacobite sympathiser because it threw its rider even before reaching the Ford of Frew and then plodded its own way home.

Perhaps the horse had sensed the presence of 'calthrops' on the ground. These vicious little pointed iron spikes lie almost invisible on the ground but are quite capable of laming a horse. The approaches to the Ford had been liberally sprayed with these devices in an attempt to delay the Jacobite army. They probably would have succeeded without the intervention of Robert Forrester of Wester Frew. He knew the way through the lethal spikes and offered to navigate the Prince around the hazards. His offer was gratefully accepted and the Jacobite army moved successfully through this major obstacle on their way to capturing Edinburgh and the successful battle of Prestonpans.

Although not many locals took part in the rebellion it was still considered a good spectator sport. Several residents went to watch the battle of Falkirk and were almost caught up in the fighting. Spectators James and Henry Grahame of the Brae of Cessintully (both members of a family with strong Jacobite sympathies) were rather unlucky because they were captured. James escaped but Henry was taken north by the Jacobite Army and allegedly was in captivity at the time of the battle of Culloden. Such was the harsh punishment meted out to the 'rebels' it is not inconceivable that Henry was an active combatant but understandably used this ruse to save his life.

8

In the Centre?

INITIALLY, DESPITE THE POLITICAL TURMOIL, THORNHILL BEGAN to slowly grow and establish itself, but it was not without difficulties. The Napier family had failed to ride their financial crisis and in April 1704 Archibald Napier's eldest son, Alexander, sold King's Boquhapple, including the superiority of Thornhill, to George Drummond of Blair Drummond. For the next 50 years the village was to experience little growth. An early Drummond Estate rental of 1743–54 listed 27 feuars, only one more than the total in 1711. Roy's military map of mainland Scotland c. 1752 (*see Fig. 14*) showed that the village had not extended much further west than the two cross wynds. However, the base for growth, established in 1696, was established and the district looked to the future with confidence.

The main economy of the Scottish Highlands tended towards the rearing and sale of cattle for the rich markets of southern Scotland and England. This led to the development of the droving trade, in which cattle in large herds were driven 'on the hoof' from the north to the large fairs at Crieff and especially Falkirk. From the north west the main droving routes tended to travel via Aberfoyle or over the Leny Pass to follow the river Teith. From there the cattle would pass over the bridge at Stirling and onto Falkirk. Thornhill was bypassed by the Callander route for a long time, but when the Stirling Bridge tolls increased many drovers took the cheaper option and used the ancient and free fords at Frew to the south of the village. Thus Norrieston and Thornhill soon became thriving centres for the droving trade. It was a tradition to allow the drovers 'stands' where their cattle could graze overnight and several such stands surrounded the village. Drovers tended to sleep in the open with their cattle but would have made use of the numerous inns in the village for refreshment. The present buildings housing the former Crown Hotel and the current Lion and Unicorn were in

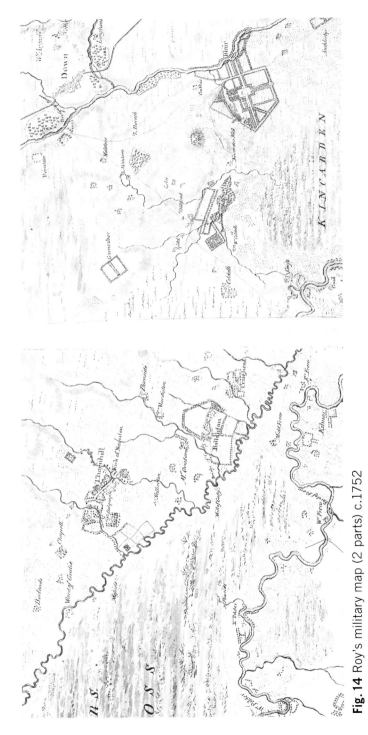

Fig. 14 Roy's military map (2 parts) c.1752

This military map was made after the 1745 Rising. Thornhill is a very young settlement at this time. The walled gardens of Blair Drummond are particularly evident.

use by this time and it is easy to imagine many a lively night in the
various bars.

The drovers used rough paths and rights of way but there were
few roads as such until 1713 when the new military road from
the castle at Stirling was built. Since 1688 Scotland had been split
by serious political rifts between the exiled Stuart Kings and the
incoming Orange and later Hanoverian monarchs. The Grahams
of Boquhapple and most of the nearby Highland Clans tended to
support the Stuart Kings. This led to unrest and local difficulties.
To 'nip trouble in the bud' the government built a series of forts
and garrisons in the heart of the troubled areas and one such fort
is at Inversnaid on the banks of Loch Lomond, the ruins of which
can still be seen today. This new route went right through the new
village of Thornhill.

The redcoat soldiers garrisoning the forts were sometimes Scots
(the Black Watch were raised for such duties) but more often than
not they were English soldiers. They were sometimes regarded as
an army of occupation, particularly as the very unpopular Act of
Union had only just been pushed through the Scots parliament in
1707. Locals must have been curious to see the 'foreign' troops frequently marching along the road, but at least new markets would
have opened up and they would have gained some welcome trade.

It is possible to begin to construct a picture of the village and
its surrounding areas at that time. Before 1760, the village houses
were little more than huts, with holes for windows without glass
in the most part. By 1790, all the houses in the village had glazed
windows. In the early days even the church was thatched. The minister of Kincardine at the close of the 18th century noted that the
villagers:

> have become a little more attentive to cleanliness than
> they were formerly, but there is still too much room for
> improvement in this article (with respect to their person!), and
> still more with respect to their houses

The layout of the village had changed little. Thornhill maintained the
original planned layout of a straight main street with feus extend-
ing north and south. It broadly followed a cruciform pattern with a

dominant Main Street and a Cross Roads. The broader open space at the Cross was originally intended to be a Market Place but this never developed as such.

The feus behind the houses gave enough space for growing potatoes and other crops and the keeping of a limited number of animals. Most of the early residents had come from a semi-subsistence background and this continued as they used their strips of land to the rear of the houses for growing crops and they grazed cattle on the North and South Commons. Some of the barns and byres, most now used as sheds, are still present to the rear of many of the houses on the Main Street and the Common lands are still in evidence. The South Common is now used as a football park and children's playground and is the site of the Community Hall, completed in 2001 after many years of local fundraising. The North Common maintained its original function as a common grazing area into the 20th century and is now valued as an area of open space for the villagers. Further Commons existed to the north of the village (the Skeoch) and down on the Moss lands but these have since been lost. Most of the older feus for properties in the village give a glimpse into a lifestyle now past as there is often a clause in the deeds which allows the use of the surrounding Commonties for the:

cutting of turf (probably for thatch), the grazing of animals and the use of the quarry for stone

The large estates were now under pressure from smaller tenants but still employed many local people and also maintained their exclusivity of grain mill usage for their estate workers. Several of the grain mills were of significant antiquity. Ruskie Mill is attested from 1507, the grain mill of Wester Boquhapple from 1536, the Mill at Cessintully from 1542 and the Mill of Goodie from 1683. Most of the people in the village were labourers. By the early 1800s Thornhill had virtually become self-supporting. The tanning industry now employed 20 men and produced shoe leather for export. The importance of weaving was paramount. Over 40 looms were in the village and it was said that almost every house was:

enlivened by the sound of the loom

Thornhill had developed a thriving domestic weaving community, based especially in Low Town and Doig Street. The cloth was woven in the home but the rise of the factory system in the late 18th century and early 19th century led to the demise of the home weaving industry. The new Deanston Adelphi Cotton Mill was beginning to grow at a tremendous rate and by the early 1790s it employed over 700 people. Many weavers from Thornhill now worked in this new factory. The walk over to the mill was long but many Thornhill residents did it twice a day, every day.

Conditions were often atrocious. The weavers' revolt of the early 1800s comprised workers who had complained of their appalling pay and conditions. The revolt was brutally suppressed and two weavers were hanged in Stirling for their 'crimes'. Circumstantial evidence suggests that local weavers may have been involved in this minor revolt. For example, a leader of the Perthshire weavers was named Sands, the name of one of the original village feuars, and at that time an important family in Thornhill.

Fig. 15 Weavers cottages, Low Town

This photograph dates from the early 1920s and highlights the poor state of the road. Were weavers from this street involved in the 'radical war' of 1820?

An early written description of the village notes that:

Most people are religious, sober, industrious and frugal but several are intemperant, with cases of fraud and stealing. This is because of the effects of distilling local whisky

Several observers had remarked upon the former activity of whisky distilling. Roger, writing in 1851, observed:

At the distance of nine miles from Stirling and about four miles from Kincardine, we reach the village of Thornhill, renowned in former times for the number of its stills, but now enjoying a reputation more creditable from its abundant supply of excellent water[25]

It is difficult to establish exactly where the stills were situated as there were very few official records kept of the industry as many illicit stills were in operation. The excellent flavour of the local blend was said to be a result of the local water, much of which came from a well at Middleton of Boquhapple. A distillery was set up here by Robert Downie about the middle of the 18th century but an Act of Parliament stopped production to allow concentration of the industry in the larger commercial distilleries. So ended the Thornhill whisky industry, but Robert Downie was to make his mark elsewhere. It was said that he made his fortune in the developing of the British province of Bengal, India and returned home to become, by 1820, the local Member of Parliament. His career took a nose dive but he was well thought of in Thornhill and this seems to have been reciprocated, as in 1815 he had presented four silver communion cups to the Norrieston Chapel of Ease.

The same chronicler who remarked on the evils of whisky drinking also noted that matters improved when whisky distilling stopped. Nevertheless, there were still seven ale houses in Thornhill and a local minister[26] complained:

These seven houses produce very pernicious effects, especially when the innkeepers are low persons

---

25 Roger, 1851.
26 Rev. Christopher Tait, minister at Kincardine, c1807.

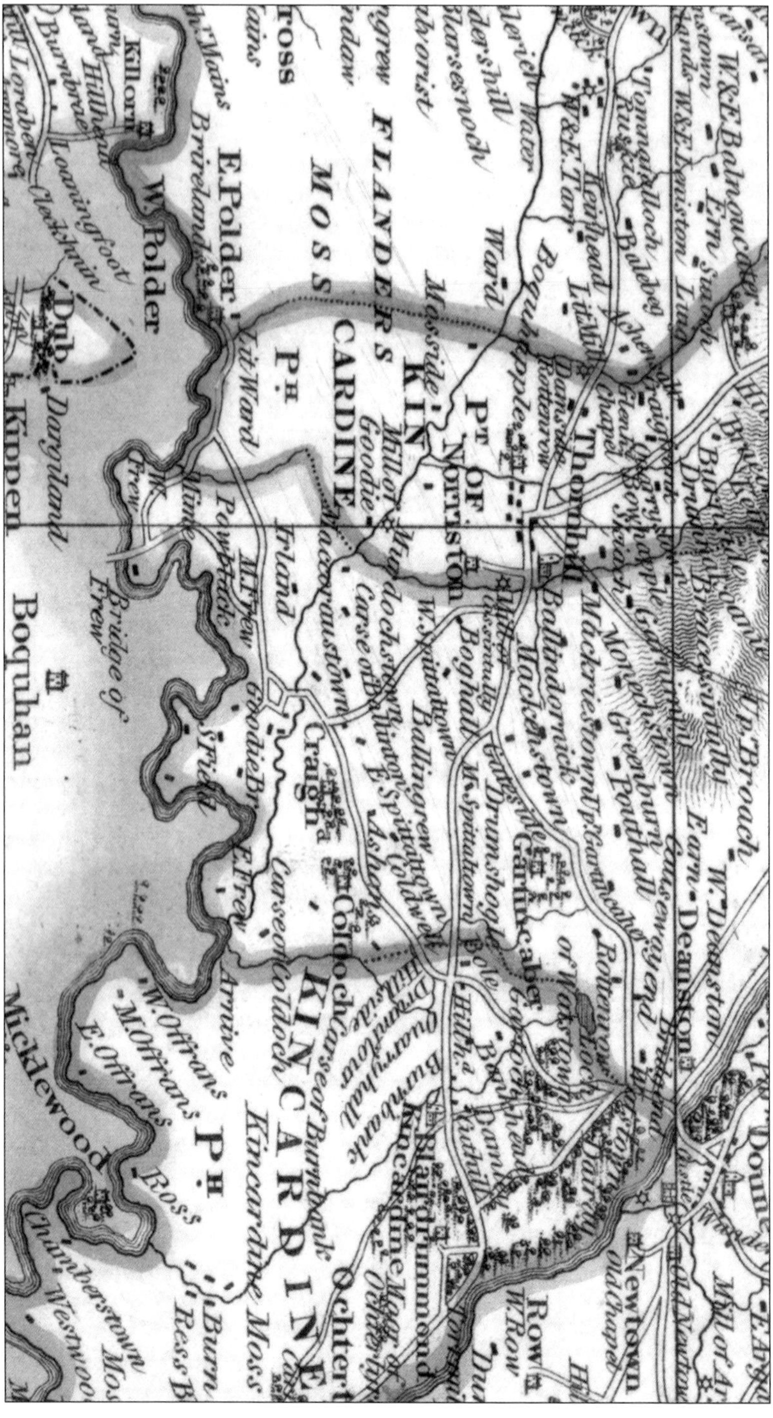

Fig. 16 John Thomson's map of western Perthshire 1832

Fig. 16 reveals that Thornhill is now a distinct route at the centre of the junction of five routes, and the weaver's row of Low Town is clearly shown. The main route south is by Craighead and the Bridge of Goodie towards Frew. The route to Callander is similar to today, but the main route north was by the Skeoch towards the Ford of Lanrick. This route has now disappeared. Note the Chapel of Boquhapple, marked just to the west of the village.

and he connected the overuse of alcohol with:

> *a want of veracity and respect for the law, intemperance, fraud and pilfering, and the habit of defrauding the government*

Not all the village conducted their business in a drunken haze. There was a parish schoolmaster and five private schools. It was noted that:

> *All were well attended in winter but deserted in summer because of the practice of the children working on farms*

The general impression of the village was, on the whole, favourable. The Reverend Hugh Laird (Minister in 1800) left Thornhill to take a charge in Portmoak and one day met former parishioner Mr MacFarlane of Whirriston. He complained:

> *Oh, it was a fine place – Thornhill. Plenty of respectable men for elders – here I can get only tailors or shoemakers*

The reverend gentleman had obviously not received very many favourable comments, especially concerning his dress sense! By the mid-19th century there were two parish schools, both ultimately to be replaced by the present school building. Thornhill was not a wealthy community but by the standards of the 19th century there were few very poor people either, with only three families maintained by the parish. By 1837 a postal service was also operating:

> *letters arrive every Monday, Wednesday, and Friday, and are*

despatched on Monday, Thursday, and Saturday afternoon at one in winter and five o'clock in summer

By the end of the 18th century the road layout was roughly as it is today although the Main Street (then called the High Street) had become narrower and was not metalled. The Hill (or Hill Street as it was then called) was then a cul-de-sac and it had still not been 'made up' in living memory. Some older residents remembered with amusement the scenes of their childhood as they watched the chaos and listened to the cursing, as horses, vehicles and people tried to climb the Hill in winter when frost and snow lay on the ground. It was even worse when the winter rains turned the area into a quagmire.

Heroes and Villains 4: *Robert Wallace*

R obert Wallace was the son of Margaret Stewart and Matthew Wallace, then the parish minister of Kincardine. He was born in the parish on 7 January 1697 and after an early education locally he entered Edinburgh University in 1711 (just 14 years old). In 1717 he, along with others, founded the Rankenian Club, a society of intellectuals, often regarded as the most important of the learned clubs and societies which were such an important feature of the Scottish Enlightenment.

In 1722 Robert was licensed as a preacher, becoming minister of New Greyfriars, Edinburgh in 1733. Robert was an original thinker and his career was noted for its controversy and unorthodoxy. Nevertheless in May 1743 he was elected Moderator of the General Assembly and in the following year he was appointed a royal chaplain for Scotland. One of his main achievements was to originate the widows' fund scheme for minister's wives, an early example of social welfare. He is chiefly remembered today for his publications on population. His 1753 book *Dissertation on the Numbers of Mankind in Ancient and Modern Times* made his reputation, where amongst many other matters it contained a learned criticism of David Hume's *Political Discourses*. In *Various Prospects of Mankind, Nature, and Providence* (1761), he expounded his population theories, and was believed to have had an influence on Thomas Malthus, the famous population theorist. He died in July 1771 aged 74.

Local life had its difficulties. The area had developed a bad reputation for rheumatism for people of middle age, especially incomers, due to the damp climate. It seemed to have less effect on the locals. Tales are told of the Earl of Moray speaking to his tenants in the Frews area in the 18th century. He saw tenant John dancing merrily on a table at the age of 70 and he said in jest:

John you are too rich and wanton. I must raise my land (rents)

John answered:

My lord, it is not the land that has made me rich, but god's providence ... and the change of wives!

Nevertheless, for most people, life remained hard and very simple. Visitors seemed surprised by the lack of servility that appeared part of the make-up of the Scottish peasantry, comparing it with the more absolute control over tenants which seemed to be the case with the upper classes of England. However, the local inhabitants had little to be proud of in terms of material possessions. Early visitors to Scotland often remarked that they were puzzled by the apparent disregard by local people for material possessions, noting especially the poverty of the houses. Froissart reported in 1385 that Scots were largely unconcerned by the burning of their homes in the English Wars, as they said they could rebuild them in three days, as long as they had some timber for the roof. Three hundred years later the houses were not much improved and most of the houses in the village were by today's standards little more than hovels.

Heroes and Villains 5: *Ramsay of Ochtertyre*

It is perhaps rather disingenuous to include John Ramsay in this volume, as Ochertyre is not strictly within the Thornhill 'sphere of influence'. However, the importance of his work and the intimate details he provides on life and work in the local area would make his omission regrettable.

John Ramsay was born at Ochtertyre House, two miles east of Blair Drummond, in August 1736. He succeeded as 'laird' of Ochtertyre when aged just 12 but thereafter soon moved to Edinburgh where he studied Classics at the University and then trained as an advocate. He obviously didn't fancy the lawyer's life as instead he returned home to Ochtertyre.

The rest of his life was spent looking after his estate and writing on 18th century Scotland. In 1785 he was elected a Fellow of the Royal Society of Edinburgh. He was a renowned letter-writer in his own lifetime and held in very high esteem by his contemporaries, as can be seen by the illustrious visitors to his home who included Robert Burns in 1787 and Sir Walter Scott in 1793. His greatest achievement was writing *Scotland and Scotsmen in the Eighteenth Century*. This epic work, which ran to 18 volumes at the time, has been described as the finest book on Scotland in the 18th century. His descriptions of farming and village life in his local area, which included the Thornhill district, make it an invaluable source for any history of the period. He died on 2 March 1814 and is buried in the graveyard at Kincardine.

The difficult living conditions surprisingly did not seem to have as much deleterious effect on health as would be expected. Records show that many people in this area were noted for longevity, a tradition carried into more modern times by the MacFarlanes of Crosshill. Crosshill (or Corshill as it is known today) was a smithy early in the 20th century, the last smith being Sandy MacFarlane. He died at 94 years old, both his parents survived into their eighties and his brother Daniel lived to 88, still shoeing horses well into his seventies. His other brother Robert died at the comparatively young age of 81, but Robert's son, also called Daniel broke the family record. He died shortly before his 106th birthday and remained active to the end. He accounted for his longevity by eating plenty of porridge and never marrying. However he was quick to point out

Donald MacFarlane

Fig. 17 Crosshill Smithy

A working scene from the inside of the Crosshill (Corshill) Smithy around 1900. This smithy was the home of the MacFarlanes, a family renowned for their longevity.

that he had had plenty of opportunity but was never tempted-not even by his housekeeper of 51 years, Miss Anne Alexander. When asked why they did not marry she replied:

he isn't my type and I'm certainly not his[27]

[27] Interview on the occasion of Daniel's 104th birthday.

9

How I wish, how I wish you were here[28]

Population Change 1755–1945

IT IS DIFFICULT TO GIVE ANY ACCURATE population statistics for Thornhill and its surroundings because boundary changes have made interpretation problematic. Most of the area today recognised as Thornhill would have been included in Kincardine parish but prior to 1891 the Kilmadock parish extended to the river Forth and covered much of the area to the east of the current village. Consequently statistics are given for both parishes. Kilmadock parish also includes Doune and Deanston, so the 'Thornhill environs' part of this parish is relatively small. This history also includes small parts of the parish of Port (the Ruskie area) but does not cover Kincardine parish where it borders Stirling and Lecropt (e.g. Drip).

There are no accurate population statistics prior to the establishment of Thornhill in 1696, the first 'official count' being 59 years later with Alexander Webster's survey of 1755. This, although not a formal government survey, gives a good estimate of population at that time. Parish Ministers were asked to provide information about the total number of inhabitants, the extent of their parish, the numbers of ministers, Roman Catholics and Protestants and the ages of the inhabitants.

The population of Kincardine Parish was then recorded at 1250 people of which 1248 were Protestants and two were Catholics. Kilmadock's population was considerably larger with 2730 people. In the wake of the 1745 rising the government was anxious to establish possible sources of future danger and so the number of fighting men were also recorded. The number in Kincardine stood at 250 with 546 fighting men in Kilmadock.

The 1801 census showed that the parish of Kincardine had an increased population, now reaching 2212 people, almost double that of 1755. Thornhill, now easily the largest settlement, had reached

---

28 Waters, Pink Floyd, 1980

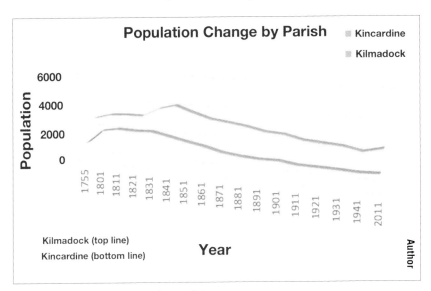

Fig. 18 Population change by parish

*This graph shows population change from the beginning of the
19th century (the first government official census was in 1801) up to
1941, with the 2011 figures added for comparison.*

a population of almost 626 people and had expanded up to and
beyond The Hill.

Kilmadock had also grown but much more slowly. It is tempting to conclude that the large population increase in Kincardine
was due to the success of the newish village of Thornhill but may
also reflect the improved gathering accuracy of the statistics. Population in Kincardine continued to rise until it peaked in 1831 at
2456 people. However, in 1861 the population of Thornhill was
thought to be 621(with 285 males and 336 females) and this number was little different from that of 1801, indicating a stalling in
growth for the village.

Kilmadock peaked in 1841 with a population then almost double
that of Kincardine. The new Deanston cotton mill was then employ-
ing over 1100 people and this would inevitably have an impact
upon the population statistics. Workforce in this mill continued to
grow for much of the 19th century reaching almost 1500, but by
the beginning of the 20th century it had declined to 500 people.
Clearly natural increase took place, as it did throughout Scotland

and the UK as a whole. However the major growth at this time was also thought to be due to immigration as a result of the Highland (and possibly Irish) clearances.

Population decline from the late 19th century cannot just be put at the feet of the Deanston mill. In fact both Kilmadock and Kincardine (note that in 1891 a reorganisation saw much of the land to the east of Thornhill moved from Kilmadock parish to Kincardine parish) experienced a steady but inexorable population decline. The lack of a railway in Thornhill and the consolidation of farms into larger units all contributed to this decline, so that by 1941 population was barely 50% of that at its peak.[29]

Emigration also played a role in population decline and there were plenty of emigration opportunities. With the growth and spread of the British Empire Scots were destined to play a big part in manning and policing the colonies. Consequently the spirit of emigration was ever present and Thornhill sent many of her sons and daughters to Canada, Australia, New Zealand and other parts.

An early emigrant to leave the village was George Moir (1784–1855). George, born in Thornhill, married Jean Stirling (1796–1867) in the village around August 1815 and they went on to have 12 children over the next 22 years. No reasons are given but with their younger children they emigrated to Usborn Township, Ontario, Canada, sometime before 1851. George was only to live another four years and Fig. 19 shows Jean in mourning.

At a similar time Duncan McGregor, a farm worker at Mackrieston and Norrieston lived at 92 High Street (the old name for Main Street). His daughter, Janet McGregor, married the Thornhill schoolmaster Archibald MacDonald and the couple, with their three children, bravely decided to start afresh in the distant and relatively new colony of New Zealand. Janet and Archibald soon found themselves on 'the Philip Laing'. This ship departed from Greenock on 23rd November 1847 and arrived at Port Chalmers, New Zealand on 15 April 1848 after a passage of 114 days. Archibald kept a detailed journal during the voyage in which he recorded the experience of passengers in steerage. His account,

---

[29] The 2011 population, inserted for comparison, shows a population increase, perhaps due to transport improvements and the rise of commuting to Stirling and beyond.

This is a very striking early photograph, taken sometime between 1855 and 1867. It is particularly interesting in view of the fact that the first ever photograph of a woman in the world only dates from approximately 15 years before this one.

Fig. 19 Jean Moir (*nee* Stirling) c. 1856

although primarily positive, illustrated the hardships of such a long voyage such as the inadequacy of the rations provided for the children. His ship was the second ship from Scotland to arrive. The first ship, 'the *John Wickliffe*', was largely for provisions for the new settlement so Archibald and Janet, along with 237 other pioneers, were among the very first settlers of Dunedin (which is the Scottish Gaelic for Edinburgh). The leader of this emigrant group was Thomas Burns, the nephew of Robert Burns, the poet. Thomas was a firm and devout churchman but a strong supporter of the value of education. He ensured that the schoolmaster Archibald, became the first schoolmaster of the new settlement and thus was central to Dunedin's growth and development.

Life in the early days of colonial development was difficult. The MacDonalds lived in a wattle and daub cottage in Stuart Street, a painting of which still survives. This housed their initial family of five plus a further ten children they added over the next few years. Relationships with neighbours could also cause problems. A court case involving them in a dispute with their neighbour George Crawford is recorded from 1859. A Macdonald hen had strayed into Crawford's wheat field whereupon George promptly shot it. Archibald Macdonald took the dead hen, beat George over the head with it and a brawl developed between the families. The Magistrate dismissed the case, but Janet Macdonald was threatened with jail 'if she did not control her temper'.

Figs. 20–21 Archibald and Janet MacDonald

Fig. 22 The first house of the MacDonalds in Dunedin, New Zealand (Note the chickens)

It was written in 1859:

> *The spirit of emigration is very popular in this area. Few*
> *villages of a similar size have given more to the British colonies*
> *than Thornhill. They are all good hardy people. A few years*
> *ago most went to Canada but now most go to Australia and*
> *New Zealand*

Perhaps to redress this balance on 1 April 1910 Mr Hugh McKerracher, a travelling emigration agent from Canada, came to the area and stayed for two days. He used an impressive and gaudy decorated wagon with good horses to strengthen his message. He exclaimed:

> *Unparalleled opportunities await young men in agriculture and*
> *female domestic servants in Canada*

He had mixed success. In 1911 a number of emigrants, such as the young Messrs. Yule and Thexton had presentations given to them as a farewell. A further five people left the village in 1912, but all to Australia. This emigration trend was to continue, encouraged by public events and films, well into the 1930s and is still evidenced today by the many people who live away from the village but keep up with Thornhill affairs via Facebook and other social media.

10

The Great and the Good?

THE HISTORY OF THE THORNHILL AREA IS much more than the history of the great landowners and statesmen but nonetheless, for centuries these people had an inordinate impact upon the everyday life of the locality.

	Pounds
Lord Kames of Blair Drummond	3072
John Ramsay; Ochtertyre	511
Lord Napier	400
Laird of Lerwick; Ruskie	385
Earl of Moray (Coldoch, Mill of Goodie)	342
Laird of Craighead, Norrieston	229
Graham part Boquhapple	194
Govan part Boquhapple	125
Robert Drummond of Calziemuck	100
Murdoch of Gartincaber	66

Fig. 23 1771 Survey of the main landowners

This table shows the rental value for tax purposes not the 'sale value' of the land, value to the nearest Pounds Scots.

Very noticeable is the continuity of ownership shown by families such as the Drummonds, Napiers and Grahams, who had owned land in the locality for hundreds of years. But the history of the people of Thornhill is also the history of the everyday life of a Scottish community and at times they seemed to show little respect for rank and pretension. This was well summed up by Archibald MacDonald towards the end of the 19th century. He met a duchess with associated retinue on a narrow bridge and was told to move aside. He refused:

Do you know who I am?

asked the frustrated duchess. Of course Archibald knew very well who she was:

Yes, but I don't care if you are the duchess from hell. I was on the brig afore you. You move![30]

I understand that she did but it would be incorrect to suppose that the folk of Thornhill had a natural antipathy to the large landowner. The Lanrick estate has already been described as a place where the welfare of their tenants and workers was not ignored. Lanrick is not considered to be particularly close to Thornhill today but until this century it was connected with Thornhill by hill routes and rights of way. An early drove route and a major route from the north used the ford at Lanrick, moved on to Thornhill and then travelled via the Bridge of Goodie towards the major crossing point of the Forth at Frew. A strategic position at the Highland margin and the Teith crossing helped the house to develop a rich history, especially with its strong Jacobite connections.

The direct route from Thornhill north to the Lanrick ford can be seen on John Thomson's map of 1832 (*see Fig. 16*) and many local people worked on the estate. The house of Lanrick stood on the site of a very early settlement, probably a tower house, but it was 'gothicised' with turrets and battlements in 1791. The interior at this time was particularly grand, although some thought rather ostentatious:

more magnificent than convenient[31]

At the time of the 1745 rebellion the estate was under the control of the Haldane family, and they raised a troop of horse to serve the Prince in his abortive campaign. The house of 1791 passed to the MacGregors, who had also supported the Jacobite cause. The house became known as Clan Gregor Castle and the impressive but not well known MacGregor Monument was built in the grounds.

---

30 Rev. Williams *Diaries*.
31 Ramsay of Ochtertyre, 1801.

Fig.24 Norrieston House

Situated in Norrieston close to the original Chapel of Ease, these listed houses – dating from at least 1757 – may be the oldest in the village. By repute this building was the traditional home of the factor of the giant Drummond Estate.

Sir Euan Murray MacGregor later sold Lanrick to Mr William Jardine MP. Jardine had made his name for his business activities with James Matheson in the Far East. They built their fortune from the Opium trade but their partnership ultimately spread to more legitimate and acceptable activities and their company grew into one of the largest trading concerns in the world.

In April 1994 the castle was gutted by fire and lost its roof. Heartbreakingly, on 16 February 2002 Lanrick was confined to history when the rest of the house was demolished, despite it being a listed building.

The Home Drummonds of Blair Drummond often exercised a paternalistic overview of the village despite some controversial claims to the common ground in the Moss. In 1840 there was a large party in Thornhill to celebrate the marriage of Mr Home Drummond younger. Eighty people attended a banquet at Lamb's Inn and there were over 25 speeches following the meal. Just three years later in May 1859 the 'new' school was being built in Low

Fig. 25 Blair Drummond House

Blair Drummond House belonged to the Home Drummonds. From the time of Lord Kames and his ambitious drainage schemes the Drummond family played a significant role in the growth of Thornhill, especially in the development of the water supply and the school buildings. This photograph shows the 'new house' of 1868 which replaced the older one designed by the Earl of Mar, a well-known architect (and leader of the Jacobite Army of 1715 in his spare time).

Town courtesy of Lord Home Drummond and following a rebuild in 1959 it is still serving its purpose well today. Overall, it does appear that the Home Drummonds were well liked. On 26 August 1830 the village held a celebration for Lord Home Drummond on the occasion of his re-election as the local Member of Parliament. They were not the only ones to celebrate because even the prisoners in Stirling Gaol sent a congratulatory address to him. Perhaps the prisoners had an ulterior motive because he responded by giving them all a very good dinner.

There are numerous buildings in the village associated with the Drummond family. Norrieston House on the Main Street, a listed building dating from the early 18th century, was by repute the tied house of the factor of the Drummond Estates. As a result there

Dating from the early 18th century this house may well have served as an early manse, and probably was the home of divinity students, once plentiful in Thornhill.

Fig. 26 Benview

would be only a nominal rent payable and as late as the 20th century the rent was said to be:

one red rose annually

Benview, situated on The Hill, dates from at least 1769 and probably earlier. The tack on the property was granted by Agatha Drummond, probably to her gamekeeper. At a later date the house seemed to be used as a temporary manse, in all likelihood for the Chapel of Ease. Hopefully not as a consequence of its ecclesiastical function but more likely because of Thornhill's reputation at this time, it was put in the deeds that occupiers were not allowed to:

sell ale and spirits on the premises!

To the north of Thornhill the Burn-Murdochs occupied the estate of Gartincaber for much of the 19th century and well into the 20th century. The Burn-Murdochs, an ancient family, traced their descent from Murdoch of Cumloch, a leading follower of Robert Bruce. Their house is not quite as old as that but the oldest part of this listed house dates from the late 1400s-early 1500s. Most of the structure was built in the 1760s and renovated and modernised in 1843. An article in the Scottish Gardener of December 1910 describes the impressive garden and trees such as the grove of lime trees planted in 1747. It also noted that on prominent display near the house was a bell and cannon ball from Sevastopol brought home during the Crimean War.

Fig. 27 Gartincaber House

This fine house has an ancient lineage. In this photograph the wing to the left dates mainly from the 18th century, the wing to the right is Victorian. The estate was once renowned for its gardens. The impressive avenue of lime trees is behind the house.

A prominent landmark on a hill nearby was Gartincaber Tower built in 1799 by William Murdoch. It was often alleged that the tower marked the geographical centre of Scotland but clearly the builder was not a geographer! William Murdoch scandalised the neighbourhood by marrying his housekeeper, Sarah and it was whispered that the tower was built for her. No-one is sure of the exact function of this folly but it certainly gave good views of the surrounding countryside. It later had a practical use, being a trig point for the Ordnance Survey and later still was used as a Second World War look-out post. By the late 20th century it had fallen into serious disrepair and was finally finished off during the fierce gales of January 2012. Little now remains to be seen.

Neil Aitkenhead

Fig. 28 Gartincaber Tower: the centre of Scotland?

Heroes and Villains 6: *Ebenezer Brown*

Perhaps if geographical advice was needed Ebenezer Brown of Braendam may have been the man to ask. This was our own local empire builder who, had he kept a diary, would have told a fascinating story of the many late 18th century activities of the British Army in Europe and the burgeoning British Empire. His military career was founded as a surgeon, first in the 79th regiment and later the 30th regiment. He went with the army to the West Indies where malaria and yellow fever were to take a huge toll of life. He returned to take part in the British invasion of Egypt. He was busy behind the lines at the battle of Maida in Sicily and then served in the hugely successful peninsula campaigns that did much to destroy the myth of invincibility that had grown up around the Emperor Napoleon Bonaparte. Following the end of the Napoleonic wars after the battle of Waterloo in 1815, he returned to Thornhill bringing with him a captured Spaniard and a bear:

Which for its tricks on breaking loose one night had to be destroyed

Hopefully he was referring to the bear.[32] Ebenezer enjoyed his retirement and tended his house (a listed building built in 1742–4 but 1790 in present form) and garden, but was always happy to revert to his role as doctor whenever the need arose. In July 1828 the local legend Ebenezer Brown passed away.

Fig. 29 Braendam

A fine listed mansion now owned by the Lilias Graham Trust. James Fairfoul of Braendam was a J.P. in the proceedings against Rob Roy's sons for the abduction of Jean Kay from Edenbelly in 1750. Later this became the home of Ebenezer Brown, his Spanish captive and his wandering brown bear.

---

[32] Just kidding, he was. The Spaniard apparently settled in the area and later married a lady from Callander.

11

'Second-to-none for well cultivated farms'

AGRICULTURE HAD LONG BEEN THE PRINCIPAL LIVELIHOOD of the majority of local people but the development of the new village of Thornhill with its markets started a new economic chapter.

Evidence suggests that from around 1750 the agricultural population actually began to decline. The fermtouns were becoming outdated and the smallholdings, really no more than crofts, were barely viable units. It was recorded that in the late 18th century the state of agriculture in west Perthshire was still primitive and in some parts still retained features of traditional agriculture, namely the infield-outfield system and runrig.

Infield-outfield involved putting all the available manure on the arable 'infield', usually close to the farmhouse. The rest (the outfield) got no manure but a part was maybe ploughed and sown until its fertility was exhausted. The outfield, not usually under arable, was chiefly used for grazing. There was a tradition that the locality was famous for cheese in medieval times indicating that livestock rearing was important, partly utilizing the grazing land on the mosses in addition to the nearer outfields, the meadows and pastures beside the streams were particularly useful, though many were boggy and liable to flooding.

Runrig, well adapted to the fermtoun layout, means that the farmland of the tenants was separated, often in strips or squares, rather than compacted, enclosed holdings. In those pre-machinery days arable cultivation remained a tough activity. Four tenants often had one plough gang between them and each sent one man and one horse to the spring ploughing. The four horses were yoked to a broad plough. One man held the horses, one drove them, and one held the plough and the fourth dug the rocky areas where the plough could not go. The land was then divided into small parcels, about 18 square feet in size, for which the tenants cast lots. Hazel or willow rods marked the borders of their allotted plots and each sowed their seed with the main, and in some cases only crop, of black oats. Evidence suggests that barley was important too, as the area had a thriving market in local whisky production.

Runrig had almost disappeared in the Thornhill area by about the mid-18th century. The great enclosure movement was gathering force everywhere as the common land and outfields became enclosed discrete units so that every tenant held his land, usually of about 50 or 60 acres, as a compacted entity. The myriad of small farms gradually became amalgamated into larger and more economic holdings and the pattern of the surrounding farms began to resemble that which can be seen today. This wasn't to the advantage of all and enclosure in addition to farm consolidation meant that there were inevitably winners and losers, with many tenants being dispossessed. Many, fearing for their future, interpreted the changes as the rich landowners using state processes to appropriate land for their private benefit.[33] Some, like James Stewart, even took matters into their own hands. James was just 19 years old when around 10 February 1831 he wrote to General Alexander Graham Stirling, his landowner.

To General Graeme of Bogtoun
by Doune and Thornhill

Dear Sirs,

*I am informing you as a friend that our society threatens
against you for your being so tyranacle (sic) and our
towns peoples fully determined not to be under such
like and you are one that is reported unto us for being a
tyrant, and if you remove any of your old tenants or make
your farms into larger ones we will come and burn up
all your premises and your barn yard, if there be any and
perhaps your own life; for it is that of supresor (meaning
suppressing) the tenant that is brought to the ... world
into such confusion. I am your determined friend.[34]*

33 Thompson (1991) argued that "enclosure was a plain enough case of class robbery."

34 NAS JC26/1831/169

He was accused of 'wickedly and feloniously composing and writing (or causing to be written) a letter containing threats'. Trial was set for 28 March 1831 in the High Court of Edinburgh and witnesses from Thornhill, notably Alexander Ferguson, a farmer of Moss-side and Walter Ferguson a weaver, formerly servant to the maltman in Thornhill, were called. However James, knowing full well the serious nature of the charge, failed to appear for trial. In his absence he was found guilty and sentenced to fugitation (becoming a fugitive or outlaw). His ultimate fate is unknown but if apprehended his best outcome was likely to have been transportation to a penal colony overseas.

Dispossession continued despite the protests and by the end of the century many of the dispossessed farmers had moved away to supply the labour for the industries of the cities that were beginning to sprout in size. Some however moved into Thornhill and began to develop new businesses and services for the surrounding population.

Notwithstanding this, another event, the draining of the mosses, was to capture the imagination of the nation and change the local landscape in a dramatic fashion. Had we eyes to see the landscape of the early 18th century it would be dramatically different to what we see today. Many areas had remained almost unchanged from the dawn of civilisation and one of these areas would have been the great moss that covered much of the headwaters of the Forth. 3000 years ago this area was a secluded arm of the ocean and formed a shallow sea. Fine muds were being laid down in the quiet waters and further proof of the sea presence can still be seen in the frequent beds of shells found on the carse. One very thick bed was found at the Bridge of Goodie. Also, in 1824, the bones of a large whale were found near Coldoch and were kept in a museum in Blair Drummond.

Falling sea levels led to this shallow sea area becoming land and it was soon occupied by a thick layer of forest with oak, hazel, alder, birch and willow. Some of the oak trees were immense and during clearing in 1793 one oak trunk was 4 feet 8 inches in diameter and in 1823 another was found which reached 16 feet in circumference. It appears that the forest was felled by Agricola during the brief Roman occupation of the area, probably because it gave such good shelter to the pugnacious Caledonians in its midst.

The whole area even today is still only a few feet above sea level and in our wet climate it gradually developed a thick bed of peat which was of very limited agricultural value. This low area, when surveyed by Winter in 1754, was described as consisting of 2000 'useless' acres of 'The Great Moss of Kincardine' and 'The Drip Moss', surrounded by small, tenanted farms between the Mosses and the Rivers Teith and Forth.

It was incorrect to state that all the upper reaches of the Forth and Teith consisted of 'useless moss'. Gaps in the peat moss had enabled agriculture and settlement to exist for hundreds of years. Furthermore the moss itself was used, albeit on a limited scale.

When the moss was drained and demand for agricultural land increased there were many disputes concerning ownership of what had been considered 'commonty'[35] lands. Court cases were the result and full statements were often taken from people who worked in the area, thus giving us an invaluable insight into the way of life of farmers and residents from the late 18th century.[36]

Many of the early 19th century witnesses from the Boquhapple and Polder Moss areas stated that the main value of the moss was for peats. However, it also had a limited use for cattle grazing. For example, Paul Doig, a tenant in Moss-side of King's Boquhapple in 1810, retained land next to the moss which belonged to Lord Drummond. Paul's family had worked this land for very many years. He commented that:

he herded his father's cows when he was young ... all the tenants herded their beasts on the moss together ... asked if the cattle which pastured the moss had other pasture in the low ground ... it was just as the people chose to allot it for them, that it was the yeld cattle [dry cows] that were pastured on the moss and the milk cows on the low grounds and ... some of the tenants had one or two sheep that went to the moss with the yeld queys; asked if the pasture on the moss is of any value

35 Land which belonged, in common, to adjoining landed proprietors who (via their tenants) had customary rights to use the land.

36 The important 2003 study, 'A historical background of Flanders Moss' by J.G. Harrison and commissioned by Scottish Natural Heritage gives a very detailed picture of this and documents a number of local cases.

he said that it is certainly of some value ... that in wet weather there are some parts in the moss in which cattle are apt to lare (get bogged down)

It was known that underneath the peat was potentially rich agricultural land and attempts at the systematic clearance of parts of

Fig.30 Henry Home, Lord Kames *by David Martin*

the western carse lands had been underway from well before the mid-18th century. The main tasks were to get rid of the peat and to keep the existing land dry by installing good drainage.

In 1766 Agatha Drummond and her husband, Henry Home Lord Kames, inherited the estate of Blair Drummond. Lord Kames then launched upon the most ambitious clearing and draining scheme yet attempted in the area.

Lord Kames' idea was to simply remove the peat (sometimes lying up to 12 feet deep) thus gaining access to the fertile soil beneath. He began his scheme by cutting a three-mile ditch, which would take flowing water across the Carse from Blair Drummond to the Forth river and thus begin to drain the wet moss.

The surrounding lands were let to incomers in 10-acre blocks, each block linking with the ditch. The new tenants were required to cut cubic blocks of peat, throw them into the ditch, and float them to the sea. Lord Kames offered these tenants a lease for thirty-eight years. They were to be provided with timber to build a house and enough oatmeal to sustain them for a year. They would pay no rent for seven years; in the eighth pay one merk; in the ninth, two merks; and thereafter they would pay 12 shillings for each cleared acre and 2 shillings and 6 pence for each acre of moss. This seemed a decent deal, as good farmland then averaged a rent of 30 shillings.[37]

Until the peat had been removed there was little point in erecting wood, brick or stone houses, so the following method of construction was adopted:

> A deep trench was first cut in the moss and carried down into the clay below the peat. In the centre was left a large block of solid peat the same size as a house. Then the house itself was scooped out of this block, rather like hollowing out a turnip on Halloween. The walls were four feet thick at the base and three feet at roof level and timber was used for the roof. As the peat dried out the walls contracted so that a room originally 12 feet high ended up as five feet high!

No doubt this played havoc with the interior decoration schemes.

Life presented major challenges for the people living on the former moss lands. By 1811 there were 764 people living and working on the moss and almost all these new settlers were Highlanders. They were tough, often wore Highland dress and spoke Gaelic, many not having any English at all. However, the popular image of the 'wild highlander' was not well founded in this case. They were known to be sober, frugal and industrious and it was noted that there was not one reported instance of theft or any other misdemeanour amongst them and not one of them claimed Poor Relief.

The new tenants faced the backbreaking work of stripping the low moss using muscle power alone. Firstly they were instructed to construct peat-walled cottages within the depth of the moss itself and as such had to live in very damp conditions. This was replaced at the earliest opportunity by a second home. This was better, usually made from supplied timber or brick (from the nearby Blair Drummond brick works). The first tenant took up the enterprise in 1767 and by the time of Lord Kames' death in 1782, there were 42 families working on the moss, 37 of them from the Perthshire Highlands. 336 acres had been let and approximately 80 acres in total had been fully cleared and were producing their first crops. Progress nonetheless was slow.

---

37 There were 12 pennies to a shilling and 20 shillings to a pound. A merk was worth 2/3 of a pound.

Lord Kames' and Agatha's son, George Home Drummond, continued the project and aimed to clear the remaining High Moss and the Flow Moss, often nearer the centre of the Carse and at least twelve feet deep, often more. He knew that if the scheme was to succeed, it would need many more tenants, better access roads and a larger and more reliable water supply. The labour supply was the direct result of warfare, social change and agricultural change. Many of the clans of Perthshire were solidly Jacobite, and they suffered heavily in the aftermath of the 1745 rising. Most of the leaders lost their land and the ordinary people found that their paternal clan system was broken, never to return. The overcrowded Highlands could no longer support such a large population in the prevailing peaceful environment and many looked towards the nearby lands for work. The Balquhidder and Strathearn areas had a number of dispossessed estates and were able to provide a significant number of the new settlers who found their work in the clearing of the moss.

The settlers were called moss tenants, or very often the tongue in cheek, 'moss lairds'. Their plots were accessed by a twelve-foot-wide road dug down to the underlying clay and crossing the Carse between twelve-foot-high walls of peat and moss. The first areas of moss cleared was to the east of Thornhill on the estates between Blair Drummond and Stirling. Soon clearance spread to the moss to the south of Thornhill itself.

The early methods continued the approach pioneered by Lord Kames. A trench was dug down through the peat to the clay below. This trench was made into a channel that ran north to south and led into either the Goodie or the Forth rivers. The tenants would loosen the peat either side of the channel and throw the turfs into the water to be washed away downstream. This relied upon an abundant source of water and unfortunately this was not always present. Nevertheless, clearance in this way continued in the wetter areas until the 1860s. At South Flanders and south of Thornhill, areas where water was relatively abundant and labour would otherwise be a limiting factor, small moss settlements (the 'Pendicles') were constructed. Despite all of this, the work could still only proceed in winter due to the low river flows and thus the settlements remained small.

In 1783 the drainage venture took a more dramatic turn,

especially in the Blair Drummond section, and events there were to have an impact on agricultural development throughout the world. George Home Drummond had initially constructed an extended road network but still needed a larger and more reliable water supply. George Meikle of Alloa came up with the idea of a water-powered lift using the force of the River Teith to rotate a waterwheel with small upward-facing buckets on the inside of the wheel. These would discharge water into a trough at the highest point in the rotation. By October 1787 the wheel, pipes and aqueduct had been completed and installed at the Mill of Torr.

The wheel, 28 feet in overall diameter and 10 feet in width cost £1000 to build and raised 250 gallons of water to a height of 17 feet.[38] The water then went into an aqueduct 1400 yards long, which carried the water to the centre of the carse (by day) or to a storage reservoir by night. The wheel operated successfully for 61 years until 1840 and by then almost all the area had been cleared. It has been estimated that over 20 million cubic yards of moss, vegetation and ancient tree trunks had been excavated in this small time frame and almost exclusively by human muscle power. The clearances to the south of Thornhill were a little later but just as extensive:

The moss in the vicinity of Thornhill... has of late year's undergone considerable diminution. About 20 years ago the Earl of Moray raised an embankment of three miles in length to convey water from the dry field to the level of the moss and which was carried over the river Guidie by a wooden trough or what is well known by the name of 'trows'. During the winter season between 20 and 30 men were daily employed in putting away the moss; and in spring of last year the Earl had it all cleared from his estate in that quarter. There are now about 200 acres of excellent arable land converted from what was formerly covered with heath[39]

The 1811 count of the Moss inhabitants showed that in addition to the resident population of 764 men, woman and children they had

---

[38] The working prototype of the wheel, constructed by Meikle, is now kept at the Scottish Museum of Country Life, at East Kittochside, East Kilbride.

[39] September 1830, Stirling Journal.

264 cows, 166 horses, 375 hens, 30 pigs, 168 cats, and 8 dogs. By 1840 their original leases had expired but many settlers had already sold the lease at a profit once their plots were cleared. Also some put in bids to amalgamate several of the plots into larger units; out of the 50 or so houses which once existed along Kirk Lane, only two farms exist today.

Although Lord Kames and his son George were among the first of the large scale 'improvers' who introduced many new methods and ideas, they were not the only ones locally. Mr McEwan of Black Dub farm was recorded as being 'noted for intelligent enterprise' and he invented the successful Drain Plough and put it to good use on his land.

The 'improvers' were not universally admired. Lord Kames faced severe criticism from many quarters for his rather profligate waste of peat, a potentially valuable fuel and fertilizer. Additionally the moss drainage brought the whole concept of 'commonty' and 'common land' into question. In the areas south and west of Thornhill clearance was pursued with vigour but in the process almost all the common land, with the exception of the North and South Common and high up on the Skeoch, was taken into private ownership. [40] But it was not without a fight.

The 'commonty' disputes were to continue for a number of years. Between 1760 and 1780 the smaller proprietors had already started to encroach onto the moss lands adjacent to their own lands, especially on the Blair Drummond estates south of Thornhill. By 1800 the Earl of Moray also had a big reclamation scheme underway, aiming to clear 200 acres of Polder Moss. The remaining moss lands were surrounded by landowners who all wanted as much of the commonty land as possible and disputes were inevitable.

It was clear that the commonty arrangements as previously known could not continue in their present form after clearance. An Act of the Scottish Parliament of 1695 had allowed commonties to be divided amongst the surrounding proprietors. Each adjacent proprietor had to demonstrate to a court what title they had and also show that they had used the traditional rights associated with

---

40 This has remained an issue. The Skeoch is now lost as common land but ownership of the North Common was subject to dispute in the latter part of the 20th century.

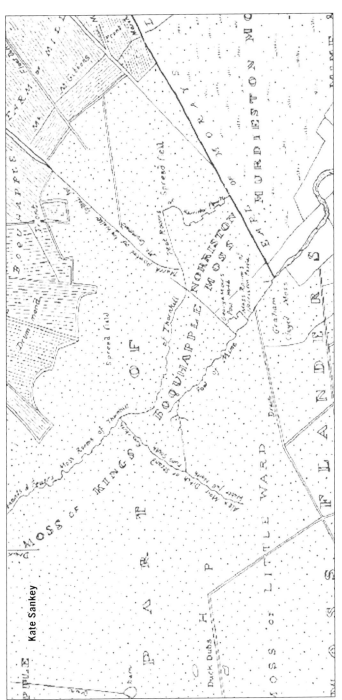

Fig. 31 Moss drainage and common ground

This early 19th century map shows the Moss to the southwest of Thornhill. To the north are the areas of land parcelled out to local inhabitants. The areas to be used by the feuars of Thornhill are clearly visible, as are the 'Moss Rooms and Peat Rooms of the Norrieston People'. This area was the site of a legal battle over common ownership of land.

the commonty, usually grazing and peat cutting. It was then up to the court to divide the land and usually each proprietor was given a part adjacent to their own lands. It then became their property to do as they wished.

However, the dilemma was to establish the proportion to be received by each of the proprietors. Was it according to the proportion of use they had made of it in the past or how much of their property encroached on the periphery or perhaps it was the total value of their holding as compared with that of their rivals?

The last option meant that a large estate which made minimal use of the commonty might obtain the major share and that was often the option sought by the larger estates such as the Drummonds. There are records of a serious dispute in 1806 over the Commonty of Boquhapple Moss and the Poldar Moss, consisting of 438 acres between the Goodie and the Forth. Lord George Drummond was opposed by John Paterson of Easter Moss-side, John McCubbin of Moss-side, John Buchanan portioner of West Moss-side and David Forrester of Polder. These disputes were not solved until 1820 and there were hundreds of pages of evidence produced. A final agreement seems to have been arrived at privately and the result is unclear and could be called a draw. Nonetheless, the years of legal dispute provided a test case into the rights of the smaller tenant farmers in dispute with large landowners. The power of the large landowners was curbed to an extent but in the process the whole area was divided, enclosed and the common ground lost forever.

Clearances in the Flanders Moss area to the west had also taken place but work finally came to a halt in 1865 as apparently the dumped peat had silted up the Forth and caused problems further downstream. By this time over 10,000 acres of the Carse of Stirling had been cleared, leaving behind the zone which now forms the protected Flanders Moss. This expanse, which gives us an insight into what the area from Stirling to the headwaters of the Forth once looked like prior to its drainage, is now an area of great scientific and wildlife interest. It has regained its 'value' in a more modern way and is managed by bodies dedicated to its protection.

The developments on the Carse had attracted world-wide interest and were often used as examples of what 'enlightened' landowners could do to improve their land, becoming an element of what we now call the 'Agricultural Revolution'. They were a constituent part of a general but dramatic farming change in which fields were enclosed, new techniques were adopted and marginal land was brought into cultivation. The end result was a decline in the agricultural work-force but a massive improvement in agricultural output. The fertile and varied lands around Thornhill were ideally situated to take full advantage of these transformations.

On the 7 January 1823 a new cattle market was held in the village. Although the right to have fairs had been granted to Thornhill in 1695 they had fallen on hard times. However the rising confidence of the local farmers led to this new market being established for cattle and it was to be held on the 1st Tuesday in January and the 15 May annually. The 1823 market reported brisk trading and good prices. On 1st January 1828 the usual market took place but the cattle were of inferior quality and sales were dull with many beasts unsold. The January 1830 market saw considerable improvement. The market, taking place on the Commonties around Thornhill, reported that four times the number of cattle were sold than in the previous year. 1831 saw a downturn again in the January market with a very poor attendance and only 48 cattle on show. Unsurprisingly, sales were poor. Things recovered a little by January 1832 and cattle sales were much better. The roller coaster sales figures typically suggest that the Thornhill market was working at the margins of profitability.

In 1850 changes were made, with the market moving to the second Tuesday in March and the abandonment of the May sales which had never really been economic. Things began to look up and by 1851 there were over 200 cattle and horses in attendance. Unhappily, the long term viability of the Thornhill markets had always been in doubt, probably because of poor communications and the very large nearby markets at Crieff and Falkirk. Since 1823 the market had gradually mutated into an agricultural show and in future years this show element was to become more pronounced, although occasional cattle sales continued throughout the century on the traditional dates.

The first formal agricultural show began in July 1851. The pattern quickly became established as competitions developed across the whole range of farm animals and there were of the order of thirty separate classes to be competed for. It gives a reflection of the times that many of the competitions were aimed specifically at feuars in the village. It indicated that to keep a pig, poultry, a horse and a few cows was the norm for the village residents and the Commons would have been heavily used for grazing their stock. The show was followed by dinner and speeches, usually at Sorleys (now the Lion and Unicorn) or Hay's (probably what became the Crown Inn). Indeed this was a conspicuous feature of almost all the many and various gatherings throughout the 19th and early 20th century, in that they were followed by a dinner and usually a dance with music. It is little wonder that we hear talk of the 'good old days' when we explore the social life of those who were financially solvent. The tenth annual show took place on the 24 July 1860. It was held on the park adjoining Sorley's Inn (this would be by the North Common). For the first time some judging was held indoors in Mr Sorley's new hall, which he wanted to show off as he had had it fitted out just for the purpose.

Local farm workers were proud of their skills and rarely missed an opportunity to display them. In March 1820 an annual ploughing competition was instigated. The competition moved around the various farms of the district and no doubt few farmers objected to expert ploughing being done on their land in the name of competition. The 1820 competition took place at Mr Paterson's Moss-side and it was reported that there were a vast number of spectators. By 8 February 1826 the ploughing match was organised in the name of the 'Thornhill Farming Club' and that year it took place at Ward of Goodie. Thirteen ploughs entered, with the first prize going to James Johnston of Gartincaber. The Johnstons of Gartincaber were to dominate the ploughing competitions for some time.

In the well-established manner the farming club dined, after the ploughing, in the Monteith Society Inn (now possibly Menteith House, 33 Main Street). The annual ploughing competition has continued, with only a few gaps, almost up to the present day and the competition obviously helped to raise farming standards, as an observer of the village noted in 1861:

> *Thornhill stands second to none for well cultivated gardens and farms in the vicinity*

A sample of entries from the competition gives us a picture of the scale of the event. On the 12 February 1869 it was held at Munnieston. Twenty-eight ploughs competed, with a large number of prize winners. Overall first was David Brown, servant to Robert McGowan of Ballinton. Fifth was Andrew Paterson, ploughman to our old friend Daniel MacFarlane, the Smith of Crosshill. By 1884 there were two levels of competition, a junior and a senior. The senior ploughing competition was at Mr Paterson's, McOrriston, and the junior one at Mr Murdoch's, Boghall. There were 26 ploughs competing and it was a terrible day with stormy weather throughout. This did not deter a very large number of spectators from attending the event and maybe the attraction of the all-day refreshments in the farmhouse helped to persuade the waverers to attend. An early draw in the competition was greatly sought after as the furrows would not be quite so straight after a day of traditional Thornhill hospitality.

The ploughing competitions would have presented a real challenge on the partially drained moss lands. Even as late as 1830 oxen on the moss were shod with broad pieces of wood to stop them from sinking. Moss improvements were still continuing apace and by 1830 200 further acres of moss had been cleared around Thornhill.

Perhaps sinking into the moss was a farmer's fear that was now beginning to recede, but working with unpredictable animals always has its dangers. On the 11 July 1845 young Marjoribanks, the son of a local farmer, decided to help his father. He came to regret his helpfulness. He was leading a large calf to the Common by a rope and to ease the journey he rolled the rope around his waist and prodded the calf with a stick to get it moving. Perhaps he was too enthusiastic with the stick because the calf took off and dragged him down the Main Street. Somehow the rope got tangled around his neck and it was reported that his scalp was laid bare. He was very ill for some time but fortunately he lived to tell the tale.

Occasional grain sales also took place. This is an old tradition and Robert Burns writes graphically of the incredible scenes of drunkenness that usually accompanied these events. It is unlikely that Thornhill was an exception. On 23rd August 1851 grain sales took place at three farms. The local tradition was to have a free and ample supply of whisky at such country sales but it is reported that at this one drunkenness was not as bad as it used to be.

Perhaps this indicated a new business approach to farming. The old communal approach, often a social occasion in itself, seemed to be dying. It was noted on 23rd September 1859 that the custom of 'kirns' at end of the harvest had almost disappeared:

> *The old farmers have been succeeded by a new class who practise rigid economy with their workers. Instead of 'gude kail and beef diners' there is now an apology for a dinner, often made up only of bread and milk*

Not everybody supported the new ways and a local miller was determined to keep up the old local customs so he held a 'rantin a' kirn':

> *30–40 hale and hearty lads as ever wielded a scythe, and blooming lasses as ever lifted a sheaf came to give the miller a day's work. Grain fell fast before the scythe and was quickly sheafed by the nimble fingered lifters. By the time the sun was going down the miller's entire cutting for the year was finished*

The whole party then went to his house and had a good substantial supper. Then the room was cleared for a dance which went on with great spirit until the early hours. The miller thanked them all profusely for their work, and they thanked him in return saying that a helping hand would not be awanting on their part the next time they had like work to do'.

These new 'economic' farmers saw a gradual rise in prosperity as the 19th century progressed. Even the terrible potato blight, which was to cause so much hardship and famine in the late 1840s and early 1850s in Ireland and the Highlands, had a minimum impact on the area, although there were frequent panic reports as late as 1858 about 'disease in potatoes again'.

The majority of local people still earned their livelihood on the land, either as farm workers or small tenant farmers. Everyday life for them had not changed much despite the rapid changes in the agriculture of the late 17th and early 18th century. This was because most of the surrounding lands were still sizeable estates owned by

Fig. 32 Victorian Thornhill group

Daniel MacFarlane is seated second from the left in the front row of this impressive early photograph. Unfortunately none of the other people portrayed can be named

gentlemen farmers. The business of running and farming the land was usually left to the Factor and the Grieve.

There was also the droving trade. This important trade lasted well over two hundred years and was to continue almost into living memory. The drovers would be away from home for months at a time as they walked their cattle from Skye, Lochaber and other northern areas, heading for the markets at Crieff and Falkirk.

The life of the local farm estate workers was usually equally modest. They often had a nomadic existence tending to take contracts from the farmer for six months only and then sometimes moving on to another farm. They may have been asked to stay if they were liked but often they would move to the highest bidder-a necessity when farm worker's wages were notoriously low, even in an age when overall wages generally were depressed. For example, a well-respected worker left his employment and moved to the Lanrick Estate at the end of the 19th century. The enticement for him to move, astonishing in our age of the massive soccer transfer fee, was one penny more a week.

By 1860 the farming communities were examining ways to rationalize and improve the hiring of workers and on the 6 July a public meeting was held to discuss the possibility of an annual 'feeing' fair, to be held at the Cross (the cross-roads) to streamline the hiring process for harvest workers. It was agreed that this would be on the 2nd Tuesday of July annually. The first fair of 1861 was a great success, with many workers gaining new employment. The average wages for men were then between £3 10 shillings to £4 and for women from £2 to £2 7 shillings. No equal rights at this time!

In Thornhill's now accustomed style the evening of the first 'feeing' fair saw the 'Doune Gardeners Lodge' procession in the village followed by a concert of local talent. A great attraction was always the local favourite, Mr Robert Forrester, who excelled in telling monologues.

The feeing fair and the accompanying period of time for the farm workers known as the 'flitting' was to last well into the 20th century. Of course the 'feeing fair' was an excellent excuse for a get together and the route from the fair back to their farms was often fairly long and tortuous after a long evening's 'rest and relaxation'. The ploughmen and young farmers saw no reason why they should not get an opportunity for a break, even if they were not involved in the 'flitting'. Hence the tradition of the ploughman's picnic and the young farmer's excursion was born. The Ball and the excursions soon became an annual event. For illustration purposes, in 1883 the young farmers held an excursion to Tarbet and Arrochar with the Ploughman's Ball the following night. Forty couples attended and the dance lasted until 0500 am. The girls attracted a great deal of attention and after much deliberation:

> the girl with the brown velvet dress tied with the girl from Doune as 'Belle of the Ball

By 1887 the Ploughman's Annual Picnic had become a highlight of the year for the young folk. In that year James Stewart erected a fine decorative arch right across the Main Street outside the Crown Hotel. Then a whole series of horses and decorated cars (provided by W. McLaren of Drumore, J. Paterson of Stock o' Broom, J. McLaren of Middleton, P. Mailer of Mosside and Mr D. Stewart) were made available to carry the 60 young farmers to Loch Ard and Aberfoyle.

It was the recreational events which attracted the notice of the local newspapers but life for farm and estate workers was very hard and strict with summary dismissal always possible. Burnbank Farm was owned by Mr Paterson. He was a gentlemen farmer and the practical every day running of the estate was done by his Grieve. One morning Mr Paterson, hurrying to an engagement in Stirling, took half a pie from the pantry cupboard to see him on his way. When he returned home the house was in uproar with the maid sacked and in tears as she had been accused of stealing the pie. Mr Paterson sheepishly had to admit to taking his own pie and fortunately the maid was reinstated.

Not all the employers were mean and uncaring. A local worker was carrying coal in his horse and cart to Lanrick a few years after the coming of the Doune-Callander railway. The horse, unaccustomed to trains, took fright and reared when one of the strange new 'iron horses' passed by. The unfortunate worker was thrown off the cart and crushed under the ringed iron wheels of the cart. At least his unfortunate widow was looked after by the estate, being given a small lifetime pension and work at Lanrick.

The farming community had other challenges to face. The Thornhill weather was as unpredictable then as now. Bad weather in 1858 included a whirlwind which swept through the village and caused some structural damage. Lightning can strike unpredictably and on 26 June 1913 it did. Four heifers belonging to Mr Fisher of Easter Torr were killed by a single bolt whilst sheltering under a tree. This reminded the older residents of the equally unpleasant weather of 1857 during which major disaster struck. On 5 September there was a terrible storm. James McQuarry was crossing a field just to the west of Thornhill with two friends when he was struck by lightning and died instantly, his body a charred black remnant. His two friends were also hit. Luckily one was just stunned but the other lay motionless and was given up for dead. Amazingly he recovered.

The area also suffered periodic flooding. On 22nd January 1909 much of the carse area was flooded and it is reported that many farms became isolated for several days and large numbers of livestock were drowned. Fortunately there were no human casualties. The village itself did not always escape and on 26 August 1910 there was serious waterlogging in the village with the Burnhead and the Tannery houses being completely flooded.

Today there are many impressive gardens in the district and this reflects the long tradition of interest and expertise in such matters. By the end of the 19th century the cattle markets had completely given way to horticultural interests. On 27 November 1891 30 people met, following an advert and an address by Mr R. Dawson, to form The Thornhill Horticultural Society. The group was dominated by local landowners but on the village committee was Robert Dawson, James McArthur and John Ferguson. An annual horticultural show took place in August and as usual it was accompanied by a parade led by bands and followed by a celebratory dinner with speeches and a country dance. This quickly became one of the social events of the year.

A high standard of horticulture was the norm and Thornhill Horticultural Society founder member Robert Dawson demonstrated the skills and high standards to be found when, in September 1899, he won a number of prizes at the Glasgow Horticultural Show, then the leading show in the country. It would be interesting to see if any of the present day aficionados can match some of the achievements of their ancestors. On 26 September 1890 John Johnston, a slater living in the Tanneree, had a hen who regularly laid an egg, mostly every day, with an average weight of 4 oz. (113.39 grams) and measuring 9 inches (23cm) longitudinally and 6.5 ins (16.5 cm) in circumference. Mrs McQueen of Doig Street went one better in 1907. An egg laid by a hen belonging to her was sized 9 inches (23cm) by 7.5 inches (19 cm) and had another complete egg inside it! Equally impressive was the 3 pound (1.36 kg) potato lifted by Mr Dougal of Mid Borland in October 1913.

12

The Victorian Village

B Y THE MID-19TH CENTURY THE VAST MAJORITY of the current houses on Main Street had been built, although there were many more shops and services to be found. The number of licensed premises had declined to just two, the Crown (a listed building and now a private home) and the 17th century Lion and Unicorn, which bore the name of the Commercial Hotel. The village post office was then situated in the nearby house of Slatehaa but it was to move its location three times over the next 100 years.

There were two schools. The present site of the school was in use at this time, although in earlier times Number 2 Low Town, the house across the road, had acted as the main school. This school was operated under the administration of the church but an unendowed second school called the East School was situated where the present car park now stands opposite the Scout Hall.

The Aberfoyle Road was known as Shuttle Street, reflecting the weaving industry that had become prominent in the village. This is probably where George Spittal had his workshop. Getting bills paid was just as difficult then as now, as shown by a letter sent in 1830 from a Mr Buchanan to George Spittal:

> George,
> I believe you are in much need of your money and I confess that we should have paid you before now – and we would have done so too – had we money to dispose of – this you may believe for it is a fact. It was not for want of desire then to pay your money but want of money that was the cause of this delay.

Mr Buchanan offered to pay £7 immediately to be sent by carrier from Doune and the rest at some time later. Unfortunately we have no details of George's reply but we can imagine it!

Shuttle Street was dominated by the tannery, along with a

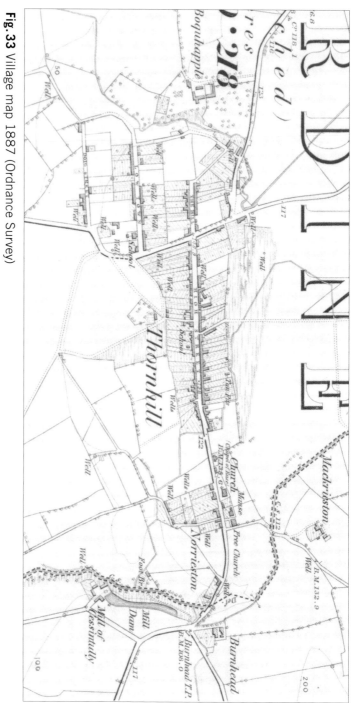

Fig. 33 Village map 1887 (Ordnance Survey)

The main street of the village was then named High Street and Shuttle Street with its Smithy is also prominent. Note the two schools and the number of wells, especially those at the bottom of the feus by the road and the South Common.

number of nearby cottages, now mainly demolished. A path linked Shuttle Street, as it still does, with Low Town. Back Yetts was not yet in existence but there were at least four houses along the path by the burn. The Low Town felt almost separate from Thornhill as it had its own distinct community, well established in the large feus that served as crofts for the inhabitants, a local school and its own water supply from wells.

Indeed most of the residents of the village would have still been involved in a subsistence form of agriculture. Many had other occupations but almost all would have kept a few animals, grown corn and potatoes, and made use of the common grazings around the village. A map of around 1812 (*see Fig. 31*) shows some of the parcelled out land on the mosses to the south of the village. Marked clearly are the lines allocated to feuars of Thornhill, Norrieston and others for the cutting of peat. It refers to 'peat rooms' and these may be the lines where peat was to be cut. It may also mean temporary dwellings used by the villagers to stay in when cutting the peat, rather like the shieling-type sheds still seen today in parts of the Western Isles.

To the south of Low Town was Doig Street. It is likely that this was a new street in the mid-19th century although some of the houses pre-date this. By 1887 there were six clear blocks of houses/cottages, likely containing multiple families (*see Fig. 33*). The name of this street reflects the long association of the Dog/Doig family to the area.

As the 19th century progressed the housing had improved and the average income gradually rose with a corresponding improvement in cleanliness and modes of living. The community was also pulling together more now helped by the moss farmers who had gradually integrated into the local community. Sadly, one result was that by 1840 Gaelic as a spoken language had almost completely died out locally. Nevertheless, the last native Gaelic speaker in the district died as late as 1937.[41] It is likely that this person would be able to trace his/her origin to a 'moss laird' incomer. In fact this descent can apply to a number of local families right up to the

---

41 Even well into the 20th century there were still 32 Gaelic speakers in Kincardine Parish and 131 in Kilmadock Parish (including one person who did not speak English).

present day. [42] One can only speculate upon what happened to the original 'moss lairds' but we know that many of them came from the Balquhidder area and shared a limited number of names, the most common being Stewart, Ferguson, MacLaren and McGregor.

The tracing of a family tree is a fascinating study. An early house builder in Thornhill was Alexander Stewart. In 1797 he built a house, now numbered 92 Main Street, on the site of a stable and brewhouse (likely an illicit distillery at this time) and another house, now numbered 79 Main Street, on the site of waste ground. He also

Fig. 34 Sands' shop around 1900 and the Buchan connection

The two houses to the left were probably built by Alexander Stewart in the late 18th century, and it is likely that the cottage to the right was also built by him. Alexander Stewart was the great, great grandfather of John Buchan, 1st Lord Tweedsmuir. The shop on the left is called Slatehaa and is by repute the first house in the village to have the luxury of a slated roof. The shop and post office belonged to Mr Sands, and this family owned a number of properties on the main Street at the turn of the present century. Note the building, now demolished, on the site of the Lion and Unicorn car park, and the narrowness of the road at the entrance to the village of Thornhill.

---

[42] Hendrie, 2004, comments that it is now considered a mark of honour to be descended from the original 'moss lairds'.

Fig. 35 The Main Street at Slatehaa, 1904

The house to the front left was probably built by Alexander Stewart. Note the Victorian widow's dress worn by the lady to the right. At this time the pavements, the responsibility of the house occupants, were in a very poor state of repair, especially on the north side of the Main Street.

owned (and possibly built) the house called Slatehaa (once known as the slate hall). It is likely that Alexander, or his father, may well have been one of the original moss lairds who 'made good' and built their permanent dwellings in the growing village. This family can be traced into more recent times. It is likely that this Alexander Stewart married Catherine Ferguson and had a daughter called Catherine. Catherine married a local man, descended from a family of small tenant farmers, called John Buchan. Their son, born in 1811, was also called John and became a lawyer and bank agent in Peebles. He was heavily involved in the City of Glasgow Bank failure of 1878 but as he had inherited his grandparent's properties in Thornhill he was able to borrow money from the Commercial Bank using these properties as security. He thus saved himself from bankruptcy in the crash. His grandson, born in 1875, was also called John and he was to achieve great fame and fortune as the author of *The Thirty Nine Steps*, *Greenmantle* and other adventure tales. He was knighted for his efforts and this John Buchan was to become the first Lord Tweedsmuir and Governor General of Canada.

13

Communications and the Tuneless Piper

THE GEOGRAPHICAL LIMITATIONS OF THE MOSSES, the rivers and the hills presented serious challenges to the traveller and communications and transport had always been major issues, especially as they had improved little since medieval times. There was strong local pressure to improve the appalling condition of the roads but when the military road was routed through the village, matters seemed to be improving. An early map of the area showed the military road to Inversnaid (*see Fig. 14*). There was no road linking the now sizeable settlement at Low Town to the Main Street, and Doig Street did not then exist although there were some weavers' cottages situated there. Equally there was no road to Frew and Kippen apart from the tortuous route via Cessintully Mill and Ballinton. The main route from the north came from the Lanrick Ford over the Teith and into the west end of Thornhill, probably where the North Common joined the Callander Road. Unfortunately this road has now disappeared but certain parts of this route are still rights of way today. The route into Stirling was completely different from today until Blair Drummond was reached, where the main route basically followed the path of the Teith as far as Drip Bridge. The road between Callander and Thornhill was said to be barely passable, and quite impossible in winter. The road south to Frew was not much better.

The problem was that good transport facilities did not come cheap and there was an understandable reluctance to provide roads which strangers could use without charge. The turnpike system met these difficulties as capital could be raised, road builders could be employed and the cost of building and maintaining the roads could be met by the collection of tolls. The draining of the moss had a useful spin-off as a new turnpike road was constructed along the north side of the moss thus helping Thornhill to communicate with Stirling. When other new roads were constructed in the early 19th century it must have been a revelation to the formerly isolated

Stewart Campbell

Fig. 36 Toll Road cottage

This pleasant cottage was originally built to control access to the Thornhill-Doune road and the occupants would also take responsibility for the upkeep and maintenance of this road. Turnpike roads were a major step forward in opening up rural areas, but Thornhill remained relatively isolated throughout the 18th and 19th centuries.

villagers, although no doubt visits to Stirling would have still been infrequent and a rather special occasion. Most people would rarely need to leave their own parish boundary but for those who did the new road linking Thornhill to the Bridge of Frew and Kippen was a toll road, as was the road to Doune. Indeed the Toll House still stood at the road end opposite Burnside Cottage until it was demolished in 1935 and the Toll House at the Doune end of the road is still to be seen, although now in poor condition.

Visitors, if they could afford the tolls, were welcomed into the village from the east by the twin carvings of a piper and a drummer and these became well-known landmarks. They were originally constructed on an old arched entrance into the former Napier estate of Ballinton but were moved in the 1770s. They were later mounted on either side of the small bridge at the entrance to Thornhill. Alas, vandalism even then was not unknown and both statues were pushed off the bridge. The drummer was broken beyond repair

Fig. 37 The Thornhill piper

An excellent photograph of the Ballinton piper minus left leg.

but the piper survived minus a left leg. Thousands of visitors to Thornhill would see the figure of the piper at the entrance to the village. He is playing an early instrument which was a mix of the Highland Pipe and the Lowland Pipe; the instrument being mouth blown but having two drones from a single stock.

So, it would have been a gross exaggeration to state that good communications had been a characteristic of the local area but strategic access to the Frew river crossings and later the military road to Inversnaid had ensured that Thornhill did at

Fig. 38 Piper's Cottage

This attractive cottage – at one time part of the entrance to the Napier estate of Ballinton – once displayed the Ballinton piper. The piper was removed to the Abercairney Estates.

least feature on major cross country routes.

By the middle of the 19th century a new mode of transport swept across the country. In the 1840s and 1850s there had been a frenzy of railway building in Scotland and it seemed that Stirling was becoming a focal point. It was considered essential that if a settlement was to grow its economy it needed railway connections. The first nearby main line, the Forth and Clyde Junction railway, came in 1856 and crossed to the south of the Forth river. Its route travelled from Stirling via Gargunnock, on to Kippen and Buchlyvie and finally to Balloch. A junction railway was opened in 1858 which connected the Port of Menteith and Aberfoyle to the line. In the same year a further line from Stirling, the Dunblane, Doune and Callander railway, was opened to the north. But no line went to Thornhill.

This was a severe blow for those who wished to develop and grow the local economy. It was partly mitigated by a regular coach service which ran along the turnpike road from the Commercial Hotel to the station at Doune but it could not provide the impetus

Mary Diggens

Fig. 39 Coach/taxi to the railway station at Doune from the Commercial Hotel

The well-dressed coachman is Mr William Dawson, with Mr Sorley looking on.

for any larger scale enterprise to develop. A newspaper article of 1885 maintained that:

> *Thornhill is unknown to many because of its difficult and poor*
> *access… If you have not been there I would say go at once.*
> *As a health resort Thornhill is foremost … and all the people*
> *require to make their village a busy one in winter and well*
> *frequented in summer is a railway*

Once more Thornhill seemed to be 'on the edge'. On the positive side however it meant that urban growth was limited and today the village is much admired for its retention of the traditional design plan laid out by Archibald Napier in 1696.

14

That Would be an Ecclesiastical Matter[43]
The Impact of Religion

IN THE LATE 16TH CENTURY SERIOUS CONFLICTS began to develop concerning the type and administration of organised religion. In 1584 James VI had reintroduced an episcopal system of church government for Scotland, a similar model to that of England and his son, Charles I, continued this trend. However, much of Scotland favoured a Presbyterian system of governance. When Charles I tried to impose upon Scotland a Book of Common Prayer in 1637 it sparked serious rioting and led to a formalised opposition in the form of a National Covenant. Support for the Covenant grew under the leadership of James Graham, 1st Marquess of Montrose and supporters were called 'covenanters'.

According to local tradition[44] an early Norrie (an ancestor of Gabriel of Norrieston) tried to rescue a minister and campaigner for the covenant from arrest, but he was brutally killed by soldiers somewhere in the Moss below Boquhapple. No doubt this hardened the strong religious beliefs of the district and in the 18th century numerous religious sects grew up to fight the established church.

It has been noted that the area was a 'covenanting' district. However, subsequent events would question this conclusion, notably the close ties of the Grahams of Boquhapple with the Marquis of Montrose, the royalist leader in the Civil War and later the local Jacobite activists following the Glorious Revolution of 1688. The Napiers, who exerted a strong local influence, were also strong supporters of the Marquis of Montrose. It is tempting to assert that the opinion of local men and women did not really matter much when assuaged against the local landowners and the 'movers and shakers' of the period. Nevertheless there is evidence, albeit of a later period, that the people of Thornhill and its environs embraced the religious controversy with enthusiasm, as it was noted that in the

---

43 Father Ted, BBC Sitcom.
44 Rev. Williams *Diaries*.

1780s a third of the population of Kincardine Parish were seceders of various kinds; a very high local percentage.[45]

In 1695, just after the turmoil of the religious 'killing times' in Scotland Mathew Wallace succeeded to the custody of the parish of Kincardine. There was no permanent church to serve the western part of Kincardine parish so he preached once a fortnight on land given to the church by Gabriel (Gavin) Norrie and delineated by order of Parliament in 1653. Ironically Gabriel was one of the first to be buried on this land, now the churchyard, but his life's work provided a real focus for the village growth. In fact there had been local agitation for a new full church since 1649. After protracted local argument and opposition by the establishment, the new village of Thornhill finally got its new permanent church building, the Chapel of Ease, built on Norrie's ground, which opened in deep snow on 29 March, 1728.

In earlier years Thornhill had become noted as a centre of Divinity and in 1762 many students of Divinity lived in the parish. By 1790 there were few left in the area but there were two full time clergymen, a minister of the Parish of Kincardine and a minister of the Chapel of Ease at Norrieston.

By now the Chapel of Ease had developed serious problems. Local tradition says this all began when the chapel was set on fire in the late 18th century. Apparently, a passing soldier on his way to Inversnaid fired a shot into the church that ignited the thatched building and almost burned it to the ground. Whether or not this was a deliberate act of vandalism we shall never know. However tradition has it that he paid his penalty when his horse inexplicably reared near the Boquhapple Road End and threw him. His skull shattered on meeting the ground and he rose no more.[46]

As early as 1803 a report to the Presbytery noted that the Chapel of Ease was in a state of disrepair and the chapel was rebuilt between 1812 and 1815 but was never completely finished. By the second half of the 19th century local concerns about the now very dilapidated building and the astronomic cost for its repair (over £1000) were becoming critical and gradually plans consolidated for a new church. The present Norrieston Church was the result, being opened

---

45 Sinclair, OSA, 1791–9.

46 Rev. Williams *Diaries*.

Stewart Campbell

Fig. 40 The parish church of Norrieston

The church, built in 1879, is in the Early English style and is now a listed building. This shows the original land given by Norrie to the community. The main religious building of the area, the Chapel of Ease, was on this site. The earliest graves have been documented (see Appendix 1).

in March 1880 at a cost of £2150 19s and 6d., with the money being raised from subscriptions and donations. The church, designed by William Simpson of Stirling, is an admirable building designed in the 'Early English' ecclesiastical style, with a fine 90 foot high tower.

Religious controversy continued well into the 19th century and led ultimately to the disruption of 1843, in which a large section of the Church of Scotland seceded and set up the Free Church. In Thornhill there was considerable support for the new church, and as a result the United Free Church (UFC) was built next to the Norrieston Parish Church to serve the new demands. It was to remain a separate church until 1927 and was later converted into the Church Hall.

The strength of the two congregations was impressive. There were huge attendances at the weekly services and both kirks had very active choirs and Sunday schools. There was a regular series of socials, dances and picnics such as the very successful annual picnic, which went far and wide. In 1907 it visited Arran; quite a feat considering the transport available at this time.

A major role of the church was the care of the community. It exerted a very powerful influence on the everyday life of the village and in the early years tended to concentrate upon the social and moral welfare of the community. Prior to the establishment of the Norrieston Parish in 1878 much of the routine business was

Fig. 41 The United Free Church (UFC)

done by the Kincardine Parish Church. Discipline was very strict. A transgressor was dressed in sackcloth and was forced to sit on a black stool (the stool of repentance) underneath a board saying 'place of repentance'. The shame for the proud local people would have been near unbearable. Discipline was to remain strict for some time. Kirk session records of the 18th century are dominated by investigations into the moral rectitude of the parish. For example on 1 November 1858 James Lawson and his wife Margaret McKerracher were brought under church discipline for:

antenuptial fornication

They had to appear before the kirk session to explain their case. It is good to know that they were absolved from scandal at the next meeting. There were very many similar cases throughout the century. In 1862 a young girl was:

purged from the scandal of fornication

One wonders what a torture it must have been for these young people to be summoned to explain their conduct before all the church elders, especially for the unfortunate unmarried mothers, usually very young girls. It is noticeable that usually it was the girl who bore the brunt of punishment and humiliation with the father often escaping unscathed.

On researching the kirk session records it is easy to come to the conclusion that Thornhill was a hot bed of 'sin' but in fact the village was no worse than any other. Other kirk session records throughout Scotland show a similar picture. What is heartening locally was the attitude of the elders, who almost without exception gave forgiveness and welcomed the miscreants back into the fold, often giving them considerable support.

These leaders of their community were well recognised for their services. One such was James MacLaren of Middleton (father of James and Robert, architects) who, in 1859, was presented with an inscribed gold watch for:

his reforming zeal and strength as servant and master,
temperance and the moral elevation of community

The care of the poor was another major function. Initially Kincardine dealt with Thornhill cases. For example in 1728 we can read that:

Malise Graham to get winter fyre to family

To a dead coffin to Patrick McArthur his wife in Norrieston £3
Scots

Cases of genuine need were sympathetically treated but short shrift was given to those who were suspected of insincerity. An officer was appointed, called locally 'Buff the Beggar', to drive off what he considered the vagrant class of the community. The Buff were not always gentle, as they were also called 'baton men'. Mr Sands from Thornhill, a well-known local figure, served for some time as a baton man in the late 19th century.

The fund for the relief of the genuine poor was the Mort Cloth Society and the community were encouraged to keep up their Mort Cloth dues. The welfare state of the mid-20th century finally brought an end to this rather hit or miss method of poor relief.

The Ministers themselves, many of whom served the community with distinction for many years, made a great impact upon this district and have been fully documented in William King's publication 'Norrieston Church'. The ministers were not without humour. The Reverend Patrick Caldwell (minister 1775–96) was notorious for his difficult wife. One day he was the visiting preacher at Gargunnock, but clearly his mind was not completely on the job in hand. Throughout the service he continually looked nervously back towards Thornhill. When asked why he explained that it was:

In case my wife sets fire to the manse

At a service in Norrieston he thought that Mr Lennox had fallen asleep during his sermon. He shouted:

waken that cauper there

Unperturbed Lennox replied:

this cauper's no sleepin sir, jist ye stick to the point

Heroes and Villains 7: *George Williams*

One minister, the remarkable Reverend George Williams, can be singled out for his special contribution to Thornhill. George was born at Holmhead, Leochel Cushnie in Aberdeenshire in 1845. What brought him to Thornhill is not known but he did marry locally.

He became the minister of the UF church around 1879 and was to remain in service for over forty years straddling the 19th and 20th centuries.

He made his mark in many ways. He was described as a man of wide information and power of research. He was an archaeologist and antiquary (elected in 1895 to the Society of Antiquaries of Scotland) and his name has been numbered amongst the leading minor poets of Scotland. He was an enthusiastic freemason and also had scientific leanings, being an authority in botany. His publications are many and varied from 'Scottish Psalms in Metre' to the 'History of Coinage'.

Historians now recognise the importance of oral history and local folklore. The stories told may not have the support of learned written documentation but many old tales would have been lost had they not been recorded. Furthermore, whatever their origin often they would have been believed by the local community and thus have played a part in the development of local culture and society. The Reverend George Williams' *Diaries* have been an invaluable addition to the history of Thornhill and many local stories would have been lost had he not meticulously recorded them.

A charming 1879 letter from George to his sister shortly after he arrived in Thornhill paints an interesting picture of the village.

Thornhill, by Stirling, March 7 1879.

My dear Eliza,

I have at last got lodgings in a farm house called Whirrieston about a mile from the village and the church ... The turn out on the Sabbath to hear Mr Cumming and myself was very large and encouraging... finishing the services which lasted about two hours. I do not know if I pleased them or not, I think so. This country is very pretty and mild. There has been no snow seen for 20 miles round since I came here. The ploughs were going Saturday last and I believe some of the farmers are ready for sowing. The view to be had is very fine. I am thinking of taking a small cottage...I can get one cheap and with the matter of £20 worth of furnishings it might be made very cosy. But I shall want a housekeeper will you come? By the bye, I have to get up to breakfast at half past 7 and at 7 when the days get fine. We dine at half past 1, this was strange at first, but I like their early hours. The lodgings appear very comfortable. I have the liberty of two rooms, but I shall only use one, a large bed room with two windows in it. There has been flesh on the table every day since I came here, and I think I shall be at home in the house.

George died at Thornhill in 1929 and is buried in Norrieston Churchyard.

Freemasonry was prominent in the village and in the early days the connection with the church, especially the United Free Church, was very strong. Many Masonic Lodge services were conducted in the UFC as the only alternative was to travel to a neighbouring village where a lodge was in existence. In those days of difficult transport it illustrates the commitment of the masons, as the nearest lodges were at Doune and Callander and local masons were prominent in both. The Reverend George Williams was to be a leading light in developing the lodge in Thornhill and he organised a committee

Fig. 42 The Reverend George Williams, Minister of Norrieston Free Church, Thornhill (*sitting in the front row third from left*)

which approached Colonel Drummond, himself an enthusiastic mason, for a plot of land. The Colonel approved of the idea and made land at the crossroads available. George Crabbie (of Green Ginger fame) owned the nearby Blairhoyle Estate and he agreed to build a hall at his own expense on the site gifted by Colonel Drummond. The Lodge Charter was granted on 2nd February 1893 and the official opening of the Lodge Blairhoyle No. 792, preceded by a procession through the village, took place on Saturday 21 October 1893. The superb new facility gave an increased profile to the Lodge in the village and inductions were frequent and well publicised over the next few years.

Fig. 43 Thornhill west end looking towards the crossroads around 1910

A group of bemused well-dressed children look at the photographer. The view today is not too dissimilar but Hillview on the corner has changed and the house in the foreground of the crossroads has been demolished. There is, of course, no war memorial. The Masonic Lodge of 1893 is prominent to the back right of the photograph.

The building itself, reputably the smallest purpose-built lodge in Scotland, is a listed red sandstone building with a tower affording commanding views, topped by an interesting weather vane at its apex. It was built in the 'arts and craft' style and was widely admired. It still is, acting as a source of interest and a landmark to travellers passing through the village.

Thornhill also became one of the first places in Scotland where the union of the established kirk and free kirk took place. This event, which took place in 1927, was two years before the official union of the churches. The United Free Church manse was sold in 1932 and in 1937, following a period of negotiation and disagreement, the United Free Kirk, was converted into the Church Hall with the proceeds of the sale; a function that continues today.

15

Superstitions and Witches

THE INITIAL FOUNDING OF THORNHILL WAS A great success, but success comes at a price. Maybe that price was a result of dabbling in the dark arts? If the stories about the Napiers were to be believed that was perhaps the case.

Indeed, it was said that no less a person than John Napier himself owed his accomplishments to dabbling in magic and alchemy. The evidence was rather flimsy. Evidently John spent a good deal of time going around dressed in a nightgown and cap, leading some to say that he was dressed as a warlock and that he had even made a deal with the devil. In actuality such a high intellect as that exhibited by John Napier would always lead to suspicions that such intelligence could not be acquired by legitimate methods. For example, John was a most successful farmer and sympathised with a neighbour concerning pigeons who were eating his crops and offered to help. The neighbour told Napier that if he could catch the birds then he could keep them; an impossible scenario he believed. The next morning the neighbour found Napier putting the captured docile birds into a sack. No dark arts; John had just fed the birds brandy-soaked peas making them staggeringly drunk and thus very easy to catch.

Contemporaries remarked that John and indeed the whole Napier family were noted wizards and:

their necromantic power was feared by nobles as well as peasants from far and wide

The family wizardry appeared to begin with John's father, Archibald Napier, who successfully predicted to the day when Mary Queen of Scots would escape Lochleven Castle where she was imprisoned. Archibald married Janet Bothwell, sister of the Bishop of Orkney, who was said to be 'a notorious necromancer'. Another Napier – John's nephew, Richard, was known as the Warlock of Oxford.

Richard, as rector of Lynford, Buckinghamshire, was said to 'cure' his sick parishioners through the powers of his magic. John's own home at Ballinton was not without drama. Following a farmers' celebration it was commented that:

> *the devil himself in the guise of a big black dog, jumped out of*
> *one of the high windows of Ballinton following an interview*
> *with the Napier laird who had vigorously refused the terms of*
> *the contract proposed by his satanic majesty*

John and his family, were definitely on the side of the good guys. In truth, he was a very committed and devout protestant and in a writing, published in 1593, John Napier associated Catholicism and the See of Rome with 'devils, fairies and spirits of illusions' and Pope Clement VIII was the AntiChrist himself.

Local tales show how magic and the devil features frequently in everyday life. Families with their children would frequently journey through the North Common and up Nellies Glen to the Skeoch area for picnics. Apart from the fine views and pleasant surroundings the children would have been reminded and perhaps slightly frightened by the history around them. They would just see the edge of the field belonging to Hillhead Farm called the "guidane'. Our forefathers were nothing if not polite and this was one of the many cautious nicknames given to the devil himself. It was customary in this area to dedicate a field to 'the dark one' to keep him quiet. Hillhead was taking no chances as they had two 'guidanes'.

Perhaps Hillhead was just too close to Nellies Glen for comfort. There is debate concerning the Nellie who gave her name to the glen. Some say she was a serving girl from the Commercial Hotel who fell out of an upper window when watching a shooting party in the glen. A more accepted origin lies with a lady called Nellie Christie. Nellie had a house near the Commercial Hotel and was known by all around to be a witch.

The treatment of suspected witches was no laughing matter. Witch trials in Scotland took place mainly between the early 16th century and the mid-18th century. The passing of the Witchcraft Act in 1563 made witchcraft or consulting with witches a capital crime. An estimated 4,000 to 6,000 people in Scotland were tried for witchcraft in this period, one of the highest rates in Europe. Seventy-five per cent of the accused were women. Modern estimates indicate that more than 1,500 persons were executed, most being strangled to death and then burned.

There were few in the area who are recorded as undergoing a witch trial. Perhaps this was because witch trials tended to take place most frequently in those districts which had enthusiastically adopted the strict Calvinistic approach to life, whereas the local stance tended to a more mixed, tolerant approach to worship.

That didn't help Margaret Spittle. A local lady, she must have suffered terribly as she was arrested and dragged off to appear before the synod of Perth and Stirling Presbytery in 1650. She knew what the punishment was if found guilty and it only needed the testimony of local people to go against her to convince a hostile synod of her guilt. No further information is available and we do not know whether she suffered the supreme penalty of so many innocent women of that period. Hopefully she survived, because in the local Hearth Tax lists of 1694 a number of Spittals are mentioned and the family was still numerically strong, which may have not been the case if they had been shamed by a witch.

Tales tell of another local witch (maybe Margaret herself). John Miller (a Ruskie Miller) was puzzled by the unexplained continual loss of cattle. He decided that dark forces were to blame and said:

They were witched, but I did for the blasted witch in the long run

He cut the heart out of one of his dead beasts and stuck it full of nails, pins, and needles and put it in his peat stack. The heart disappeared after a time and the witch never bothered him again.

The witches were kept at bay by the application of many local superstitions. Not all of them were involved in the fight against the dark forces and many impinged on normal life. The bell, rescued from the old Chapel of Ease, was believed to have special properties. In the 18th century it was said that a woman called Mary Brown could tell by toll of the Norrieston Bell when there was going to be a funeral. She was kept busy because another common superstition in Norrieston was that deaths always occurred in threes. Pigeons were useful birds, used for target practice and for supplementing dinner. Early tradition gives them another function. Apparently the Moss of Boquhapple was a favourite site for adders. A man was bitten and John Marshall was sent to find a live pigeon. The unfortunate bird was then torn to pieces and the warm flesh applied to the wound to extract venom:

> *The flesh of the gentle dove is totally antagonistic to the poisonous venom of the viper's brood*

It is nice to report that the man recovered speedily and splendidly. Had he not he may have joined the legion of local ghosts. One dark and windy day the horses from the regular mail coach to Aberfoyle appeared back in Thornhill with their harnesses broken, only a short time after passing through the village. A village posse set out to investigate and found the mail coach overturned at the side of road by the Mollins, a short way along the Aberfoyle road. The coachman had been robbed and murdered. The murderer was never caught and the mystery remains to this day. However a postscript to the story is that several sightings of a mysterious coachman in recognisable period dress have been seen in the area. Perhaps this apparition is well acquainted with the friendly spook often said to be busy behind 15 Main Street, or perhaps he prefers the phantom said to be continuing its activities at Hillview or the Spectre demonising a house in Low Town?

Heroes and Villains 8: *Robert Kirk (1644–92)*

Strictly this minister of Aberfoyle resided outside of the local area but it would be wrong to omit the man who had such an impact upon contemporary local life at the time. Additionally he had strong local connections too, as between 1648 and 1675 his father James, (and possibly Robert himself in later unrecorded payments) received his stipend of £134 Scots from the Grahams of Boquhapple and Patrick Menteith.

Robert was responsible for producing the Bible in Scottish Gaelic which he translated from a recent publication of the Bible in Irish Gaelic. However it was his treatise called *The Secret*

Commonwealth that he is best known and remembered for. His tales, often collected at first hand, told of the beliefs of fairy folklore, witchcraft, ghosts, and second sight common in the Highlands of Scotland (and his own area) at that time. Robert collected the stories into a manuscript sometime between 1691–2, but died before it could be published. Sir Walter Scott finally released it in 1815.

Before retiring to bed, on summer evenings Robert often liked to take a walk, usually in his nightgown, on the 'fairy hill' beside the Aberfoyle manse. On 14 May 1692 his body was found lying, apparently dead, on the hill. Stories immediately began to circulate that Robert had been taken away to become the 'Chaplain to the Fairy Queen' in fairy land under the hill, as a punishment for revealing the secrets of the 'Good People'. He is buried in Aberfoyle churchyard but whether his body is there or still under the fairy hill keeping the fairy queen company is not known.

16

The Power of Learning

THE PRIMARY SCHOOL IN LOW TOWN CONTINUES to enjoy a good reputation, with older residents often looking back fondly (but with some trepidation at times) on their school days and the strict but fair teachers who guided their early years.

The school on its current site was modernised and extended in 1873 to cater for extra pupils as the Easter School had closed down. The former school house, now 2 Low Town, had become a residence but its link with the school children remained for some years afterwards, as it became occupied by a lady who made toffee and was therefore very popular with the youngsters.

The now defunct Easter School was on the site of the present car park leading down to the community hall. It was opened around the beginning of the 1800s as a place of worship for the 'new licht' Anti-Burghers and at the same time was used as a school. In 1820 the hall was purchased solely for use as a school following the uniting of Burghers and Anti-Burghers with the congregation of the Bridge of Teith Church. The school was called the Grammar School, but was usually known as the Easter School and was non-denominational. As a result of the changes introduced following the Education Act of 1872, it closed down and the building became the Village Hall.

Generally the reputation of the primary school has ensured a good supply of first-rate teachers but there seemed to be a problem in the middle of the 19th century. In 1845 a series of adverts appeared seeking a new teacher, despite there being 80 pupils at school. Internal difficulties had surfaced but the details are now forgotten. Fortunately they did not last too long and soon the school was back to normal and began to tick off its achievements. Training firemen was not one of the usual ones, but in December 1902 the boys at the school were financially rewarded for putting out a serious fire. Not too many health and safety regulations to worry about then.

In addition to putting out fires the academic achievement of pupils has been commented upon. Many high achievers have passed through the school such as the two MacLaren brothers, both of whom would feature amongst Thornhill's most distinguished sons.

Heroes and Villains 9: *James Marjoribanks MacLaren*

James Marjoribanks MacLaren was a pioneering Scottish Arts & Crafts architect who was born at Middleton of Boquhapple in 1853 from a long established local family. James attended the Thornhill village school, going on to study at the High School of Stirling. He later studied at the Royal Academy, London and in Paris. His first professional project was to design a new wing for his former school, the Stirling High School

Fig. 44 James Marjoribanks MacLaren

By 1884 James, now married with two sons, was working with Richard Coad on the restoration of Lanhydrock House near Bodmin, Cornwall. This is now a leading National Trust attraction. Whilst in the area he also worked at Bowringsleigh in Devon, and Ledbury Park in Herefordshire. There, in association with an old chair maker named Philip Clissett, James persuaded him to make some alterations to one of his designs which led to the now famous arts and crafts style of ladder-back chair.

In 1886 he won a competition to build a new wing for Stirling High School, his old school (now the Highland Hotel). James was the architect of many more well-known properties, especially throughout Scotland. However, it is his design of the unique planned village of Fortingall that is usually regarded as his greatest achievement. Tragically, before the Fortingall cottages were completed, James became ill with tuberculosis. Perhaps to help fight the illness he went to the Canary Islands and there built the Santa Catalina Hotel at Las Palmas. He was back in Scotland by 1889 and designed a new Town Hall at Aberfeldy and began designs for renovating Glenlyon House and Fortingall Hotel; but before they could be carried out he died tragically young at the age of just 37 in 1890. Apart from his own designs he is cited as a major influence on later architects such as Robert Lorimer and Charles Rennie Mackintosh

Heroes and Villains 10: *Thomas MacLaren*

Thomas MacLaren, younger brother of James Maclaren and the youngest of the eleven children of John MacLaren, a farmer at

Middleton of Boquhapple, initially followed closely in his brother's footsteps being educated at Thornhill and Stirling High School. He too qualified as an architect and one of his earliest designs was in 1894 when he designed the picturesque row of houses in George Street, Doune before escaping the Scottish climate (that he blamed for causing the death of his brother) to go on to a very successful career in Colorado. There and elsewhere he designed many important buildings and left his archive of drawings and paintings to the University of Colorado.

Fig. 45 Thomas MacLaren

He is still remembered today and the Thomas MacLaren High School in Colorado keeps his name alive.

The school reflected the village, giving a portrait of a farming based society, not one of grand wealth but one where community spirit had been nurtured, grown and flowered. Other people agreed. A newspaper report of August 1885 written by 'Toledo' had this to say:

This is the pleasantest of pleasant villages, where you will be made welcome by a host of genuine country folk … It has its famous Duig Street, 'east and west the toon', as the natives say.

The entire population possess the trait by which a true Scot is known – hospitality. Another feature is its model schoolhouse judging from the smartness of the scholars. We are at once brought face to face with the fact that the training of the children is under a real dominie of the no-nonsense sort. His neat garden speaks volumes for his interest in flora. There are great gardeners in these parts – in fact agriculture, plain or ornamental is the ruling passion. It is no wonder that everything here produced is second to none.

Not all were quite so flattering about the village. The editor of the Stirling Journal gently chided the village when in 1858 he wrote:

Our friends in Thornhill must still be a leisurely sort of race – dwelling in Arcadian simplicity unaware of railways and electric telegraphs

This scurrilous accusation was because contributors for his local news column were not submitting articles at the speed which he desired.

Maybe the success of the school encouraged further activities of the mind. One could argue whether draughts is a sport or a mental exercise but the Thornhill Draughts team, established in the 1880s, distinguished themselves in competition until the outbreak of World War One.

Lectures were also a consistent feature of the village. Every Monday evening was a 'penny lecture' covering a huge range of topics. The Thornhill section of the Young Men's Christian Association was active in this arena and by 1888 had formed a special literary association. A typical example of its activity took place in the week beginning 27 April 1888 when the local branch organised a lecture on the 'French Revolution: its causes and effects'. Two days later came a public lecture entitled 'The Barometer and Weather'. Both were very well attended.

The thirst for knowledge and self-improvement was strong indeed. The school organised, on a purely voluntary basis, continuation classes for senior pupils and those who had recently left school. They proved to be very popular; for example in 1913 there were 17 students with an average age of 13.5 years. Along with the adults of the village they no doubt made good use of the local library. There were no public or travelling libraries at this time and so, in 1892, Thornhill organised its own. It was held in the school and was open on Monday evening. The annual subscription for use was one shilling. This money, together with donations, was used to stock the shelves.

17

Fun and Games

AS THE VILLAGE DEVELOPED ITS COMMUNITY WAS becoming more homogeneous with public events and facilities growing rapidly. Maybe not all the recreational activities would be to modern tastes; John Sommers, the minister of the parish (1810–39) led a campaign against cock fighting which was then very popular in the village. This would not have pleased the schoolmaster, who traditionally had organised the betting at these events and found it a very useful addition to his salary. However the schoolmaster would not have complained too much as he also doubled as the church session clerk and thus had rather mixed loyalties.

An important day in the social calendar was Auld Hansel Monday, the third Monday in January. On this day, the 18 January 1858, a new venture, held on the South Common, burst onto the scene. It was called the Thornhill Gymnastic Games and we would recognise these as a precursor of the modern Highland Games. This first games saw the Deanston Brass Band leading a street parade (which finished up at Sorley's Inn), and the games themselves had all the components of the modern Highland Games, such as Highland Dancing (fling, swords, etc.), putting the stone, throwing the hammer, tossing the caber (William Ferguson of Lanrick was the first winner) and athletics competitions, including races for the local men and boys. There were a large number of spectators and it is heartening to report that in an age when we usually hear of factories paying little attention to their workers, the Deanston Adelphi Cotton Mill (a very large employer in the area) was closed for the afternoon. In the evening came the Thornhill Ball, held in the school. This was very successful and was attended by 60 couples. An eyewitness account said:

The lassies looked very bonnie, whose gay dresses and
blooming faces added not a little to the pleasure of the evening.
Cupid was plying his darts freely

For a time the Gymnastic games continued to flourish. On 24 January 1862 the 5th annual Thornhill Games were held. By this time there was a high standard of competition and the games were attracting people from a very wide area. As usual there was a procession after the Games to the Crown Hotel (this is the first recorded mention of the name of this hostelry) and then on to Sorley's Inn. By this time the Sorleys had built up a formidable and wide-reaching reputation for their meals. The dinner at Sorleys was excellent as usual and was followed by innumerable speeches. There seemed to be quite a talent in the village for after-dinner speaking. On this occasion we hear of Mr MacLaren of Netherton having the guests rolling in the aisles with a great comedy rendition of a traditional highland sermon. The Gymnastic Games continued to grow and by 1865 the games had become a huge success, as indeed was the ball in the evening. An immense crowd of villagers and visitors attended the events.

Sadly, it didn't last and over the next few years the games declined in popularity with the last one taking place in 1877. The accompanying Ball continued but became part of the New Year celebrations, tying in with a fair held at west end of village.

At least the athletic tradition was upheld by Thornhill's John Ferguson who, on 22nd August 1884, took part in a competition held at the West Lancashire Athletic Ground and won the half mile race in 1 minute 58.75 seconds, a creditable time even today.

We live in an age where our recreation is 'on tap' and we must admire the people of Thornhill for their enterprise in organising and running social and educational ventures of their own. The list of societies is very impressive and equally impressive is the tremendous support that most of the societies enjoyed.

The thriving music club held a number of large annual concerts and dances throughout the 19th and well into the 20th century. Frequent intermediate concerts were also held. The music was mainly classical and local singers were always prominent. Scottish songs held a universal appeal, but never let it be said that the village was parochial. In May 1867, no doubt inspired by the events of the American Civil War, a group of local youths formed the 'Thornhill Negro Troupe' to sing songs originating from black Americans.

The young people of the village also formed a flute band. Indeed there was almost too much music, as a 'grand concert and nicht of Burns', held in February 1886, had for Thornhill a poor attendance and the reason given was:

a plethora of social events in village

Yet activities were to intensify even further in the following year, for this was the Golden Jubilee celebration for Queen Victoria. National self-confidence was high, the Empire was near to its greatest extent and local patriotism certainly reflected this. Colonel Drummond treated all the village children to tea, games, etc. at Blair Drummond House and almost all the village was decorated with flags:

hardly a house in village without some mark of loyalty

On the celebratory day there was a national holiday. Pipers led a march of the local volunteers through the village and services were conducted in both the Established and the United Free Kirk. This was followed by games on the South Common rather similar to the now defunct Gymnastic Games. Banquets in both the Commercial and the Crown Hotels were given by Lord Drummond for villagers and were followed by a huge bonfire and fireworks on the common. The party was to last throughout the night.

Communal events continued to be most popular and some events were aimed specifically at the children of the village. In 1880 a picnic party, to become an annual event, was held for the local children with 140 attending. It began with a parade through the town and was followed by transport to the Lake of Menteith where the party took place.

Sporting societies also sprang up and by 1865 the Curling Club, using the 'Lug' on the North Common, had become well established. They competed against local clubs and also held a keenly fought internal annual competition. The first one was probably on 3 December 1869 with a prize of 3 pairs of curling stanes for the winners. In this year prize winners were:

1. Peter Ferguson
2. Robert Millar

3. Messrs. Sands, Duncanson, McLaren, Murray (Peter) and
   Murray (John) all equal.

The football club is still a popular aspect of the village today. It is
likely that the football club began competing in 1877 and in June
of that year the club, playing on a field at Netherton Farm, won
2–1 against Stirling King's Park. What is astonishing is that there
were an estimated 300 to 400 spectators for the game. Two years
later the team (called Vale of Menteith) played Doune and we still
have the team members:

		Black			
	Duncanson	Forrester		Jenkins	
McGowan					Dow
McLaren	Ferguson	Irvine	Dickie		Fyfe[47]

These august gentlemen may have not particularly wished the game
to be remembered as on this occasion they lost 1–0. Perhaps that
is the reason why in 1880 the football club held their annual New
Year's dance; but this time as a temperance ball.

In August 1877 a Quoits Club had been formed and played their
first match, also against Doune. This club was to see intense but
friendly rivalry against local teams for many years.

Cricket also made an appearance. In July 1907 Thornhill Cricket
Club played on a field at Boquhapple and in that year they celebrated a triumph against Doune, a match which they won by 67
runs to 17.

There was even more demand for sport. On 16 October 1908 a
public meeting was called to organise and develop a bowling green
in the village.

The golf lobby also got into the act. In September 1910 plans
were drawn up for a golf course on Skeoch Brae, close to the former
common land but now on land kindly given by James Forrester. On
20 April 1911 the new golf course opened at Mackrieston. There

---

47 The old-fashioned line up. I doubt that these players worried too much about
   4–3–3 or 4–2–4 systems.

Fig.46 The Lug on the North Common

This drone image shows the area, once used for grazing and sports, but now a recreational lung for the village.

was a beautifully decorated arch at the entrance and the opening ceremony was both ambitious and grand. However the weather, which was terrible, was to prove a bad omen. Because of lack of funds the lease on the golf course was only to run for two years and sadly, in 1914, the Golf Club wound up with its assets being given to Stirling Royal Infirmary

Shooting was a popular diversion and the annual shooting competition was keenly anticipated. The first contest was held on 1 January 1881, having been organised by Daniel MacFarlane, the Smith of Crosshill. The whole area had been noted in the New Statistical Account as being rich in wildlife, especially birds of prey. In the 1880s an excited commentator noted that:

two horned or eared owls had been spotted at mid-day on the Carse south west of Thornhill[48]

A nature lover? He goes on to say proudly that both were shot and

---

[48] It is unclear what bird this newspaper reporter had seen. The horned owl is mainly North American. Perhaps it was a long eared or short eared owl.

stuffed. Glass ball shooting also gained prominence in the area and in 1888 a very cryptic message (aimed at the minister) appeared in the local press:

warning to Thornhill sportsmen

The crack glass ball shots of Thornhill should keep a sharp lookout at present, as the 'black hen' with the short feathers is to be seen daily crackling loudly round the village[49]

---

[49] Thornhill ministers seemed to have an uncanny resemblance to birds. See Appendix 5: *The Black Swans*.

18

The Demon Drink

THE 19TH CENTURY SAW A NUMBER OF great public advances, including electoral reform and new health, housing and factory acts which all helped to improve everyday life. Thornhill had reflected this in the increase in reported public celebrations and the mushrooming of activities and societies in the village.

The Agricultural Society and the Church had already built up a significant recreational role but these were soon followed by many more. The celebrations for the New Year have their origins deep in history but had certainly not been forgotten. These celebrations, which lasted for two days or more, were marked by a great deal of good humour and occasional boisterousness but very rarely was there any serious ill humour or trouble. Nevertheless there was an element of excessive drinking and many villagers felt deep concern over this. Their response, in 1846, was to set up the 'Thornhill Total Abstinence Society'. Members agreed to pledge the following:

I hereby promise to abstain from ale, porter, shrub, wine, ginger cordial and all other intoxicating liquors, except as medicines or in a religious ordinance. Furthermore that I will neither give nor offer them to others and that I will discontinue all the causes and practices of intemperance

The first president was John MacFarlane and the treasurer was Thomas Stewart. The society proved to be very popular and was to exert a considerable influence on the village. One hundred and forty-four members signed the pledge between 29 August 1846 and 4 August 1847. The group met on the first Monday of every month and continued meeting until March 1933 although under the new name of the Thornhill Gospel Temperance Society. They organised many social events including an annual soiree on 1 January.

We hear that in 1877 the soiree was very successful and the village was:

> *animated throughout the day with some turbulent behaviour but no problems ensued and everybody was very good natured*

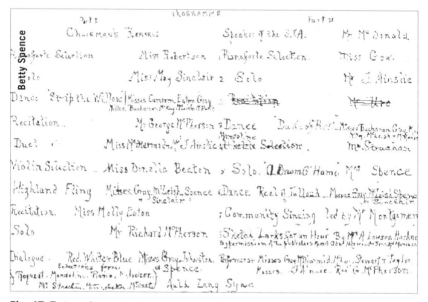

Fig. 47 Entertainment, temperance style.

This temperance concert programme of 1927 was handwritten and must have involved a lot of work for the organisers. Note the large and varied programme. If a mistake occurred then the offending word was crossed out rather than re-writing all the programmes. Almost all the entertainers were local people.

An associated society, in conjunction with the church, was the 'Band of Hope' Temperance Society, which began in 1883. It had weekly Friday meetings and the occasional social, such as the large soiree on 19 February 1884 for all adult and junior temperance band members. The Band of Hope was very well supported and by 1910 had 70 regular members and was to continue well into the 20th century.

19

Slavery, Murder and Mystery

Slavery is a weed that grows on every soil[50]

THE VILLAGE OF THORNHILL AND ITS SURROUNDING area had much to be proud of in terms of its care for the community and its cooperative spirit. But there was a darker side. Between 1700 and 1800 the British economy was transformed by the Atlantic slave trade. In 1700, 80% of British trade went to Europe but by 1800 60% now went to Africa and America, with thousands of jobs being created in Britain to supply goods and services to the slave traders. By 1783, a movement to abolish the slave trade throughout the Empire had begun to gain ground and in 1807 the British parliament finally passed the Slave Trade Act, which outlawed the slave trade, but not slavery itself. The end came in 1833 with the passing of the Slavery Abolition Act which abolished slavery throughout the British Empire and made the purchase or ownership of slaves illegal. Many of the estate owners and slave traders had made huge personal fortunes but they didn't lose everything as the 1833 Act provided compensation for lost assets (i.e. slaves).

It is comforting to know that the large landowners locally, by and large, had not become heavily involved in the trade, unlike some of their near neighbours.

Some local people did benefit financially from the compensation offered on the implementation of the Act. Matilda Graham was the daughter of James Erskine, a large local landowner. She had married John Graham of Gartur in 1800 and on his death she, after a legal battle, inherited the Three River Plantation in Westmoreland, Jamaica. She was awarded compensation based on her annuity of £500 per annum and the ownership of 170 slaves.

Caroline Robertson was another local recipient of slavery

compensation. Caroline was born in 1785 at St. Elizabeth, Jamaica where her parents owned the Bellemont estate. In 1804 she married Doctor John Robertson of Gartincaber. They seemed to split their time between their Jamaican estate and their Gartincaber home, especially on the birth of their daughter Janet, who was baptised at Kilmadock Church in 1809. John died in 1818 and was buried in Greyfriars churchyard in Edinburgh. Caroline continued to operate their slave plantation and in 1836 she was awarded £2603 15s and 6d as compensation for the loss of her 129 slaves.[51]

Crime is ever-present in every community but overall it is remarkable how few major problems occurred locally and the courts were not places towards which the village residents had a magnetic attraction. There were some domestic disputes and petty crimes but overall any problems that did occur usually stemmed from poverty or drink.

Stories tell of a serious domestic argument in the early part of the 19th century between a man and his wife in a house in Low Town. The altercation, believed to be over the wife's adultery, led to the woman running out into the garden and climbing to the top of their haystack. The man chased her and set fire to it, causing the woman to be severely burned; injuries which proved fatal. There were no local police at that time but Baillies from Doune travelled to Thornhill where, after a dramatic capture, they put the man under arrest. They took the culprit to Doune where he was publicly shackled to the cross that was then outside the Balhaldie Inn. He relied on food from sympathetic locals and perhaps it was a relief when he was taken to Stirling and imprisoned in the Tolbooth. At his trial he could well have been considered lucky to escape the hangman's noose as he was sentenced to penal servitude, spending the rest of his life in Australia.[52]

In 1902 a resident of Hill Street, in dire financial straits, appeared before a Dunblane magistrate accused of keeping an unsanitary house. His house had defective drainage, earthen floors and was damp and filthy. The house was shut up and alternative accommodation sought for the residents.

The inadvisability of drink driving is well known to us all. In

---

51 Legacies of British slave ownership at ucl.ac.uk/lbs/search
52 Rev. Williams *Diaries*.

the early 20th century the problem took on a rather different form. In 1907 John Anderson was fined ten shillings for being drunk in charge of a horse. The Sheriff said that:

fortunately the horse was well capable of looking after himself

In 1914 William Ainslie had a collision on his buggy between Thornhill and Kippen. He was convicted of being drunk in charge of a horse and fined 20 shillings or 8 days in prison. His defence was that he was short sighted and couldn't see where he was going.

A much more serious misdemeanour occurred over 100 years prior to this incident but had still not been forgotten by local people; notably the tragic events which were to overtake George McKerracher. In 1789 George was arrested and charged with rent arrears and forgery. George did not take the charge lying down and railed vociferously about the injustice of the accusation and his own innocence. His personal statement to the court shows a very articulate and determined man but perhaps rather overconfident and complacent concerning the seriousness of the charges against him. In his opinion the charges were:

Ill-founded in every view in which the case can be taken. In 1772 I took a lease from Mr James Erskine (of Cardross) of Ward of Goodie for 19 years. The farm was in a wretched condition. I enclosed, drained, fallowed and laid out crops. In time and with much experience of labour I brought it to a high state of cultivation[53]

The improvements were carried out by means of borrowing. Not all went well and he stated that:

my affairs ran into some confusion

George McKerracher owed James Erskine £17 16s and 4d for one year's rent plus the balance for the crop of 1785. George resorted to forgery to alleviate his plight. It was then shown that he had forged and distributed £48 and £49 Bills of Exchange, although

---

[53] NAS CS271/28752. McKerracher statement to the court. 22 Nov. 1789

initially he said that there was no evidence to prove this.

He went on to argue that it was the action of desperation, as James Erskine intended to end his lease and immediately remove him, his wife and four young children from his farm, Ward of Goodie. George then launched a determined attack upon what he saw as the injustices facing the tenant farmer. A tenant could be removed, lose his tenancy and his livelihood if the rent was unpaid for one year unless caution [54] is found. He argued that he would be able to find caution but was not allowed to as he was bankrupt:

> *they proceed upon an evident mistake of the case. I am in trouble for failing to find caution and failing thereof for removing … but removing is only competent upon failure of caution. But caution has been offered … this is a very great inconsistency, not to say absurdity*

George went on to make a strong political point:

> *It is no less than every tenant who holds a lease… and happens to contract debts even for the purpose of improving the farm … must forfeit the lease to his master. The law is alarming*

George McKerracher was found guilty of forgery and was sentenced to death. The death penalty for forgery was very rare in Scotland (only 26 men were executed for forgery in the whole of the 18th century) but was much more common in England. The Lord Advocate, Ilay Campbell, asserted that forgery was as much a capital crime in Scotland as in England and called for an example to be made with this execution. George still believed that he would escape the noose and argued that as no damage had been sustained by any individual he should get a restriction on his sentence. There was general public sympathy for his case. It was widely believed that he did not deserve his sentence and local tales tell of his guards offering an opportunity for escape whilst he was travelling from Dunblane Tolbooth to Stirling for his execution. He declined, saying:

---

54 Caution in Scots law is finding security against the occurrence of a certain event e.g., debt repayment.

I am innocent and not afraid to meet almighty God

He was hanged on the 28 April 1783 in Stirling. It was customary for the executed person to be buried in an unmarked grave near the place of execution but George McKerracher is buried, along with his wife Agnes Fisher, in Norrieston Churchyard. No records tell the story why, but did his burial in the churchyard reflect the widespread sympathy and indignation his execution caused amongst the good folk of Thornhill?

Part Three

The 20th Century

Fig.48 Thornhill Main Street, a general view around 1900

An easily recognisable scene today, a view of the Main Street from The Hill. The new Masonic Lodge dominates the foreground. The War Memorial is not yet built but would occupy the land shown in the bottom lefthand corner. The house on the righthand corner of the crossroads, for a long time a post office, has now been demolished. Note the state of the pavements found on The Hill. No doubt it was a matter of considerable scandal for the young lady in the centre of the picture to be riding a bicycle in these pre-suffragette days.

20

Halcyon Days

THE DAWN OF THE 20TH CENTURY HAD no significant impact on the village. New Year celebrations were rather lively but for most it was business as usual. A few novelties began to appear. In June 1902 the children were delighted to hear the church bells ringing because it signified the end of the Boer War and this meant a day off school. They were not to know that a far more terrible war was looming on the horizon. Few others suspected that either and they looked to the future with optimism as the standards of living in the village gradually improved. Only in May 1902 had laundry carts commenced a regular village visit and the myriad social occasions over the year gave a welcome break from the daily grind.

A new type of entertainment also made a big impact. In May 1902 the Northern Cinematograph Company entertained a large audience in the village hall who were thrilled by the moving pictures and the piano accompaniment. Local musicians did not feel too threatened by this advance and in March 1908 a leap year dance took place, heralded by songs from D. Donaldson and P. Yule amongst others. It is likely that Duncan Drummond, fresh from his success in national piping competitions, gave a tune or two as well.

King Edward VII almost made an appearance too. He visited Dunblane at that time and many spectators from Thornhill made the journey to see him in coaches hired from Mr Ferguson of the Crown and Mr Sorley of the Commercial Hotel. The village was gaily decorated even though the king was not coming to Thornhill, but those that went to Dunblane reported that they had obtained an excellent view. There were other visitors to the village though, such as Mr Ord Pinder, who brought his travelling circus to the South Common. Unfortunately torrential rain fell all day and the event fell rather flat.

As militarism grew throughout Europe the only signs of increasing tension locally could be deduced from the setting up in 1908 of a local territorial force. This was only a small advance from the 'volunteer E company' raised as long ago as 1891 and tenaciously promoted by Sergeant Moir, despite him being assured that the company would most certainly collapse within three years. The militarism at large certainly did not seem to dampen local spirits for investment when the properties of William Sands, including ten properties on the Main Street, were sold in Stirling in 1908. Local bidding was intense and the properties were sold on average for between £100–£200.

Fig. 49 Thornhill east end, 1920

Note the water pump in the street and the old weighing shed by the Commercial Hotel.

The fateful year of 1914 began well in the village. A super celebration on Hogmanay 1913 had as its attractions a conjurer and a ventriloquist and was followed by a dance, with Robert Dawson as MC, which lasted until 3 am. The social whirl continued for some time. On 15 January the Church of Scotland Choir held a social and dance with over 80 people in attendance. On the 5 February the turn came for the United Free Church Choir to have their social and over 70 people attended. The ploughing society held their annual competition on the 12 February with the usual social and dance to follow. Whist, which was very much a craze at this time, always attracted good numbers and on 5 March there was a whist drive and dance in the Commercial Hotel with over 70 people present. The usual Young Farmers Picnic and Ploughman's Ball were great successes, as was the Horticultural Show. The social whirl was to continue almost unabated throughout the lovely weather of spring and early summer.

20

Lest We Forget

MOST BELIEVED IT WOULD BE 'Over by Christmas' when war with Germany was declared at 11pm on the 4 August 1914. Few thought that it would become a global conflict to exceed in size and horror anything that had gone before.

The village threw itself enthusiastically into the war effort. Many men and boys (the minimum age was 18 but many boys lied about their age)[55] were in reserved occupations such as agriculture but even so they flocked to join the voluntary West Perthshire Recruit Battalion of the Black Watch (Thornhill section) raised by J. Muir.

Those who were unable to enlist began to find other ways of helping the war effort such as fund-raising. A public meeting to raise finances for the Prince of Wales Relief Fund was well supported and within a month 50 pairs of socks, 4 mufflers and 7 shirts were sent off to France. There was no ploughing match that year, the first cancellation for over 50 years and many of the regular social events were to be suspended for the duration. Despite that, the fund raising efforts continued unabated with the children sending socks, etc. to the front and organising two school concerts for Belgium. There was a pleasant surprise on Christmas Day 1914 when the children whose fathers were on war service received a present courtesy of the United States Government. That spurred them to renewed fund raising efforts and in January 1915 alone over £54 was raised for the Prince of Wales Relief Fund.

In the village a territorial regiment camped in a field by the Commercial Hotel and regularly held marches down the Main Street. They requisitioned the horses from the Commercial Hotel and when the regiment left for the front the horses went with them. Almost all the men and horses were later to become casualties. Further grim realities of war were brought sharply into focus when news came of

---

[55] It is calculated that about 250,000 underage boys volunteered, either by lying about their age or by giving false names, to which recruiters often turned a blind eye. One of these underage boys was John McLachlan, 16 years old.

the first local death when, in May, Sergeant R. Milton Hamilton of Skeoch View was killed. Although he did not belong to the village his close relatives all did and he was well known by all.

Heroes and Villains 11: *John McLachlan*

O ne can imagine that John McLachlan threw himself wholeheartedly into the social life of the village. He was not a native of the village as he was born in Glasgow then moved to Thornhill as a young boy, staying with his uncle on the Hill. He went to school in the village and when he left his uncle managed to get him a farming job at Goodie Bank Farm.

When the First World War broke out on 4 August 1914 there was great excitement throughout Scotland. Optimism was running rampant and it was confidently expected that the great adventure would be over by Christmas. The temptation was too much for the sixteen year old John and he ran away to the recruiting office in Perth. Like many of his contemporaries in the village he joined the Black Watch and was placed in the 6th Battalion. He was destined not to return home by Christmas. He spent a few months in Dundee in training at the Black Watch depot and on 22 April 1915 his battalion, soon to become part of the 153rd Brigade of the 51st (Highland) Division, was moved for further training to Bedford, England.

Even official histories accept that the Division was never really up to speed with the necessary training, facing a shortage of ammunition amongst other things. The Division was graded at average 'territorial efficiency' but the lack of training did not stop them being placed in the front lines in France and Belgium.

They landed at Boulogne on 2 May 1915 and as part of the Highland Division they were hurried to the defence of Ypres. The enemy had attacked on 22 April 1915, using poison gas for the first time and all available reserves were deployed to stop the Germans taking advantage of their initial surprise. The Division then remained in France and Flanders and took part in The Battle of Festubert. Results were not encouraging. The Highlanders were still "practically untrained and very green in all field duties," according to First Army commander, Sir Douglas Haig.

Shortly after this unsuccessful action the Division moved south to the area north of the River Somme. They relieved a French Division and became caught up in the Second Action of Givenchy. The action on the 15 and 16 June 1915 was again a costly failure. British losses totalled 3,009 and Canadian losses (for just two days fighting) were 802.

These losses were horrific but young John, despite his battalion's inadequate training, had managed to survive. Breathing a huge sigh of relief, he was moved along with his battalion to what was expected to be a quieter area. There were no assaults to be made or repulsed although exchanges of artillery fire were routine. On 3 August a Black Watch soldier reported leaving his trench to fetch water. In his absence a mortar scored a direct hit. When he returned he found the section commander and four of his men dead. One of them was John McLachlan. He was just 17 years old.

Fig. 50 John McLachlan

John is commemorated on the village war memorial along with a further 20 of his friends and colleagues who also lost their lives in those dreadful five years; a very hard toll for a small village like Thornhill to bear. The estimated male population of the village in

1914 was 190.[56] 21 sons of the village lost their lives[57] and for British troops in the conflict the numbers injured in battle were statistically almost double that of deaths. Therefore in total 63 men of Thornhill were killed or injured in World War One; this would be approximately a third of the total number of males of the village. As many of the other males would be too young or too old to serve, the figures illustrate the utterly devastating impact of the war on a whole generation.

Tragic news of Thornhill's sons and husbands was all too frequent over the next three years, following the horrors of such battles as the Somme and Passchendaele, but those at home had to continue normal life as best they could and they didn't get it easy. Many worked in the Deanston Mill and it was considered quite normal for mill workers to walk over the moor to the Adelphi Mill, do a long day's work, and then walk home afterwards.

The customary social life was severely dented by the war and events normally had a fund-raising aspect to them. In August 1918 a series of concerts for the armed forces was organised by the Reverend Mitchell but by now there was a severe shortage of home-grown talent. The problem was alleviated by using artistes from amongst the young ladies employed in gathering sphagnum moss[58] from the undrained portions of the carse.

Financially things were very bad. Although Thornhill, being a country district, escaped the worst of food rationing, many people suffered from severe poverty. One must have an element of sympathy for a lady whose husband was at the front. She lived at Mucklehoney, 39 Main Street and was found guilty of ill-treating her five children by not giving them enough food and clothing and living in a verminous condition. She received 21 days in prison. Housing standards too were still poor. Many of the houses on the Main Street were empty and many others were fairly basic dwellings

---

[56] In 1861 Thornhill had 285 males. The overall population loss for Kincardine parish between 1861 and 1911 was almost a third. On the assumption that Thornhill saw an equivalent population decline this would suggest that the male population of the village was around 190.

[57] Some accounts give the figure as high as 26.

[58] Sphagnum Moss was widely gathered and used in the manufacture of wound dressings.

with beaten earth floors. A story is told of a small family, a couple and their infant, squatting in one of the houses. When they left the house was inspected and there was nothing left in it. The young couple had even cut every other beam out of the ceiling for firewood.[59]

It was not all bad news. Thornhill had something to celebrate on 8 August 1918 when John Miller (Royal Scots), a son of the Millers of Spittalton Farm, returned home. A German prisoner of war, he had been captured when his ammunition ran out during the big German advance of 1918. He and an accompanying Russian soldier escaped from near Cologne by travelling at night and hiding by day. He lived off the land, swam rivers and had numerous adventures. Finally a thunderstorm allowed them to slip unnoticed through the German guards and over the frontier into Holland from where he returned home to a hero's welcome.

Following the armistice of 11 November 1918, the soldiers gradually began to return home and tried to get back to a semblance of normality. It must have been very difficult for some, such as Gabriel Newton of Low Town. He was gassed in 1916 and wounded twice more during the war but still survived to tell the tale and became one of the most popular characters of the village in the post-war years.

---

[59] William Ritchie, memoirs told to Thornhill Community Trust 2006.

22

A Land Fit for Heroes?

T HE PICTURE OFTEN PAINTED OF THE INTER-WAR years tends to give the impression of a village where poverty and squalor were never far away. This may be the official picture but local residents had a very different memory. The fact that the railway never came to Thornhill meant that its growth was modest and by 1935 the population was only 650. Its relative inaccessibility meant that community spirit, developed and nurtured for over two hundred years, remained strong. Mutual support, whatever form that might take, was considered quite normal and people went to extraordinary lengths to give aid when it was needed. They knew that in turn they would receive equal help and assistance and often all that was necessary was a 'thank you'.

The very high level of social activity had already emerged as a feature of Victorian Thornhill, but this did not die with the turn of the century. Dances, socials and community meetings of all types remained an integral and important part of village life and even today a relatively high level of social involvement remains. Of course there were disputes, but the abiding memories of residents tend overwhelmingly to be of good times, a happy and friendly people and a village at peace with itself. That is not to say that the area did not face huge challenges.

Water, Water Everywhere and not a Drop to Drink?

Post Great War Thornhill's story is one of consolidation and a gradual upgrading of amenities and services, but the improvements were to take time and did not appear without a struggle.

To be fair, local services were not the top priority in people's minds immediately after the war. The first priority was to erect a memorial to honour the dead. On 15 May 1919 there was a public meeting to choose a suitable War Memorial. On the 30 October

1920 the selected War Memorial was unveiled by the Earl of Moray with a guard of honour of local soldiers, commanded by Mr Kilgour, the local schoolmaster. It was a touching ceremony for all the village and there were few dry eyes as the piper played a lament for the fallen. Returning local soldiers were then treated to a formal welcome home party funded by a number of local events organised specifically for such an eventuality. It had already been decided by the Duke of Atholl, the Lord Lieutenant of Perthshire, to present a captured German field gun to the village in recognition of the local efforts during the war and to honour the 26 men who made the supreme sacrifice on the battlefields of Belgium, France and Turkey. This was placed alongside the memorial and remained there until September 1936 when it was removed for scrap metal, apparently because the wheels were rotten.

Mary Diggens

Fig. 51 The War Memorial in the 1920s

This pleasant open scene is very different today as the view is now restricted by buildings and trees. The German field gun was to remain on this site until 1936.

Thornhill had been renowned for the whisky distilling industry and its excellent quality water. It was recorded in 1744 that Mr Home

Drummond, at his own expense, brought a first-rate supply of the famous spring water by pipes directly to the village. A storage tank was built to the west end of the North Common and a series of pumps were installed in the Main Street and in the Low Town. It is claimed that as a result Thornhill was one of the first settlements in Scotland to enjoy piped water from one of the many wells and hydrants placed at intervals along the street and by the commons.

The iron pumps were notable for having lions' heads but alas they have now all disappeared. On the Main Street long arm pumps gave a supply of water. Low Town residents were more fortunate because the head of water was such as to allow them just to turn a handle and enjoy a gravity-fed water flow. However, there was no water supply installed in the houses themselves and this development was to take some time.

Much of the water supply still came from other wells. The most prominent line was to be found at the bottom of the gardens of houses on the south side of Main Street. Here, at least five wells adjoined the common land. Another major well was opposite 'Piper's Cottage'. These wells would have been social centres for the village womenfolk, perhaps only matched by the washing area at the stream to the western end of Low Town. This 18th century equivalent of the launderette was in a quarry by the Boquhapple Burn and provided a sheltered site for the washing. Fires were built in the base of the quarry and water was heated for the washing of the blankets and woollen goods. The nearby bushes and trees were used as drying posts and it was necessary to get there early on good washing days to make sure that there was still space on the shrubbery for the drying.

Also, courtesy of the Drummonds, was an improved water system introduced in 1836 and said to be a present from the laird to the village to celebrate the coming of age of his son. Cynics say that the water supply was needed to quench the thirst of the villagers following young Drummond's 21st birthday party.

The problem of Thornhill's domestic water supply became a big issue as the 20th century progressed. It was first raised as early as 1899 but it was not until April 1921 that it was seriously discussed by Perthshire Council. The local complaint, as previously mentioned, was that water was not in the houses but only obtainable from the street pumps. At least a gravity supply now served some of the village but some people still had to pump up the water a total of eight feet. The Drummond system of 1836 was now old and leaking badly, especially the Kennedy Well at the school and the Dastry Well in the North Common. It was to take 18 years of hard debate, innumerable public meetings, and tenacious lobbying by the council representatives before a new supply was finally installed to serve the houses of the village. It appeared in April 1939 and used water from three reliable springs. There was new piping throughout, and the whole system benefitted from a large new storage tank situated on the Skeoch to the north of the village.

Agriculture

Agriculture remained the cornerstone of the local economy but it was changing rapidly as the break-up of several of the big estates of the locality proceeded apace. Blair Drummond was broken up from 1912 onwards and sale particulars for the lands of Boquhapple, Whirrieston, Thornhill, Norrieston, Netherton, Moss-side and others, all of which then belonged to Captain W A Stirling Home Drummond, appeared in 1920. The farms to the east of Flanders Moss (Moss-side, Mill of Goodie, Norrieston and Littleward etc.) were also sold over the following years. Similar measures were occurring in the Ruskie estates, where a group of farms along the northern fringes of the Moss were all sold around 1930. The population was not greatly affected by these sales because most of them were sold to sitting tenants. However, this broadly set the pattern of the smaller self-contained owner-occupied farms which was to remain the basis of the ownership pattern to the present day.

The inter-war years were difficult ones for farmers and the depression of the late 1920s and the early 1930s affected them all. The government was aware of the danger which such a depressed state of agriculture could present to food supplies (and thus to national security) in the event of war. Consequently they took some remedial action, such as the creation of 'producer marketing boards', guaranteed prices, quotas, subsidies and some import tariffs. No doubt they helped local farmers but the events of 1939 were to impact enormously on food production and the threat of Nazi disruption to imported food supplies made effective home food production critical.

Tinkertown

But there was still a great deal of poverty, especially during the years of the depression. The returning soldiers had been promised a land fit for heroes but the reality proved rather different. There was just not enough money for the improvements needed in the village. During the recession of the 1920s and early 1930s water supply was not the only problem as the council recognised that many in the village were very poor. Average household rates were

Fig. 52 Hillview

This listed building has a strong claim to be one of the oldest existing houses in the village, being situated at the top of the ridge and at the junction of routes. Near this house were the 'feeing' fairs of the last century and the cross (crossroads) was the traditional place where important news was announced. The house itself has had many functions, not all legal, although it is as a boarding house early this century that it was best known.

comparatively low indicating locally poor amenities, and 24 people were getting poor relief of one sort or another. There were five official 'resident poor'; two were living on the Common, two on Main Street and one in a lodging house.

The village had also become a mecca for travelling people and others who had fallen on hard times. Hillview (*see Fig. 52*), commanding the top of the Kippen Road and the village crossroads is a fine listed building (now converted into two separate houses) dating from the 18th century. In the early 20th century this was used as a boarding house for those in transit or of no permanent abode. There were also other houses in the village which were used as boarding houses or were subdivided into very small dwellings, providing what today we would consider to be grossly overcrowded conditions.

Nos. 37/39 Main Street (*see Fig. 53*), an 18th century listed building, once housed a number of colourful characters. The house itself was once five separate dwellings, let out to tenants. People remember

Fig. 53 37/39 Main Street

A candidate for one of the oldest houses in the village, but most likely dating from the 1780s. The house, now extensively altered, is a listed building which once housed almost 20 people in five separate let dwellings.

a boot and shoe repairer called Tom Dow and for a long time the lane across the street leading to the South Common was known as 'Tam Dow's Loan'. He kept up a small garden there and woe betide anyone who picked his flowers. Also living in the block was Kenny the Painter, who is remembered as a fine craftsman who specialised in gilding. Kenny thought nothing of walking six miles to work and another six back again in the evening, and he still had time to show off his prowess at ice skating by cutting his name with his skates on the ice rink with impressive accuracy. Also fondly remembered was 'Bassie' who sold ice cream as he travelled round the village on his donkey. If that was not enough, a small antique business also operated from a base in the building.

Overcrowding was not just in the houses, with the two Commons both facing difficulties. It was reported in 1926 and again in 1928 that gypsies from far and near were parking with caravans on the Common. Twenty-one feuars complained of the dirty conditions resulting from this. In 1929 the scale of the squatter problem on the Common became clearer as it was chronicled that 5 horses, 12 men, 10 women and 23 children lived there with 32 of them in tents and 13 of them in vans. Additionally, of course, there were no services such as water, sewage disposal or power available to the squatters. Indeed, a complaint to the council said that a plague of rats was in evidence and was getting into local houses. There was some action taken to sort out the squatter problem but complaints still surfaced from time to time. In October 1930 Mr Duncanson, a council representative, noted that a horse belonging to a hawker was tethered on the Common but it was later removed. In January 1931 it was reported that tinkers with 2 boys and a horse were living in the quarry. The council had by now become less sympathetic and rather stricter in their regulations and they were moved on.

Waste disposal was another problem. There was no formal collection of household waste and it was disposed of in an ad-hoc manner. The Commons took the brunt of the waste. In July 1934 the first 'scavenging' district group was set up to arrange for suitable waste disposal and it was agreed that refuse would be collected and disposed of twice weekly and any suitable rubbish would be spread and buried on the Common or in the quarry. Unfortunately the quarry itself was almost totally filled in, mainly from waste ash from the houses. The Common itself was to be improved by the spreading of the existing dumps and the burial of tins, cutting of thistles and nettles, etc. There was also to be clearing and improvement of the ditches as the North Common still took a large part of the village sewage. Despite this, the village would still have to wait some time for a proper sewage treatment plant and for mains electricity.

Tourism

Private car ownership enables many Thornhill residents to travel to work in areas beyond the village. However public transport is less convenient. It has never been easy, although bus routes used to serve the village much more frequently than now and coordinated their services with the trains at Doune and Kippen. The Lion and Unicorn Hotel (The Commercial Hotel until 1951) had a number of stables. The Ferguson family (who owned both hostelries in Thornhill in the early part of this century) instigated a horse bus service which ran to Doune Station twice a day. This was no doubt very useful to local inhabitants, but it served another purpose in that it brought tourists to the village. Most visitors were Glaswegians escaping from the city for short breaks and the Commercial and Crown Hotels were frequently full to capacity, especially during the Glasgow Fair. Perhaps it was the difficulty of getting accommodation or perhaps it was the welcoming nature of the village, because a significant number of houses on the Main Street became owned by Glasgow people and were often used as holiday retreats. The peace and quiet of the village and its alluring scenic surroundings would have been the main attractions for the tourists but there were some other enticements. The house at 55 Main Street was the Bank of Scotland (*see Fig. 54*), but was also used as a small private museum with mainly ceramics on display.

Other diversions existed, for both tourists and locals alike. There was the bowling green next to the Commercial Hotel, opened by the Fergusons around 1912. Nearby, where now stands Norrieston Place, was a putting green. In the cold winters, a curling pond was in full use on the 'Lug' on the North Common. Indeed the curling hut still stands as a small brick building at the bottom of a garden

Fig.54 55 Main Street

The former Bank of Scotland was also once a small ceramic museum.

Fig.55 28 Main Street

Formerly the British Linen Bank.

to the west end of the North Common. The Commons themselves were of great value to local and visitor alike despite the squatter problems. Many residents still exercised their ancient rights and used the land for grazing and herding cattle, especially the North Common. A converted barn which once housed six cattle can still be seen at the west end of the North Common.

There was still grazing on the South Common too but recreation was becoming more important. The Common was badly drained and the open ditches were not ideal for developing the silky skills we now associate with the football team. The dependency culture played no part in 1930s Thornhill and locals, all volunteers, got together and formed what became known as the King George V Jubilee Committee. They had the task of levelling and draining the Common, and forming the children's play park. By June 1936 John Miller on behalf of the football club got permission to tile and drain the Common for a permanent pitch. Thornhill FC play on the South Common to this day, although the actual site of the pitch has changed.

Hamish McLachlan

Fig. 56 The football pitch
The local boys are enjoying a game, although those in bare feet may regret the heavy leather ball. In the left background can be seen 2 Low Town, one of the oldest houses in the village. The scene up to the Main Street is almost unchanged although it cannot be so easily seen today.

The South Common is now split by warehousing and the Community Hall but on this site was once an orchard. Winters were cold but at least some of the summers were hot and there was a roaring local trade in strawberries. Thornhill was noted for soft fruit production and the area to the west and north of Hill Street was all strawberry fields. This provided a useful source of employment for the youngsters of the village. The fields were busy by 6am in early summer with children picking the fruit prior to going to school. William Ure at Cambo Cottage, Low Town, was the gathering centre for strawberries and soft fruit, but here the owner boasted of a new innovation … greenhouses. Early fruit you may think, and indeed there was, but during the Second World War he found another rather novel use for his glasshouses … it became a boat building centre, and a number of lifeboats were constructed. Where were the boats launched?

Shops and Services

When the Easter School building ceased to be a school in 1872 it became the village hall. This old hall, called the Montgomery Hall, was used for anything and everything. Meetings, concerts and the weekly hugely popular moving pictures packed the hall. It served its purpose well; at least until the time came for the village dances. They were always popular and the building rocked with the energetic strains of strathspeys and reels. The building was not the only thing that rocked, as many unfortunate heads were to be equally stunned by collision with a pole which stood in the middle of the dance floor. The local technique was to avoid the pole during particular wild flurries of such dances as 'strip the willow' and the 'eightsome reel'. Alas, the technique, honed through years of experience, tended to fail as the evening wore on.

By 1937 the old building was beginning to feel its age and there was a public meeting on whether or not to purchase it for the village and continue with it as the village hall. The decision was positive and fund-raising began immediately for its renovation. The 1939–45 war came a little too early, because the hall renovation work ceased for the emergency. The hall was still used though and continued to stand the pounding of the village dances. It served its purpose well until it was used to billet the visiting troops. The troops lived, ate and slept in the hall and to do this they built ablutions at the south end of the building. It was clear by the end of the war that something was amiss. It was suspected that the building of these ablutions had undermined the wall and this was confirmed in dramatic fashion – in 1947 the whole wall fell down! This spelled the end of the Montgomery Hall and the building was demolished and the land is now the car park.

Shopping and services were much more in evidence too. There were two banks. The Bank of Scotland has already been mentioned (*see Fig. 54*) but this was in competition with another bank, the British Linen Bank, at Osborne House (*see Fig. 55*). At various times during this century other shops have included the Sands' General Store and the Post Office at Slatehaa (*see Figs. 34 & 35*). The Post Office later moved its position to the corner house on the crossroads on the south side (now demolished during road widening), before moving to 54 Main Street. The small building at the top of the loan to the South Common was purpose built for the task but it is now disused. 69/71 Main Street served as a general store and bookmaker, with a grocer at 41 Main Street, a further grocer at 34 Main Street and McLaren, the butcher at 44 Main Street. Alas, there is now no butcher in the village but the last one, Alexander Gray, occupied 47 Main Street before moving to a site on the eastern side of the loan (now called Gray's Loan) to the North Common (*see Fig. 57 on the ne page*). Prior to this, it was probably a chemist at the end of the 19th century.

The killing of animals was done in the village and there were three killing houses. One was by Gray's Loan to the North Common with, on the opposite side of Main Street, a second one at the bottom of the loan to the South Common. The Commercial Hotel had their own behind their premises.

It was even possible to buy all your clothes in the village at McNab's the Tailors, situated on the Main Street near to where Dykes Chain Saw and Lawnmower shop now is. Fond memories are given of Johnston's Newspaper Shop situated where the garden area stands today at the centre of the village by the sun dial.

Fig. 57 Gray's Loan

The road, now called Gray's Loan, forms one of the entrances to the North Common from the Main Street, and may be one of the original 'cross wynds' of 1696.

Johnston's Shop was a wooden construction built in the style of the settlers' houses of the American 'wild west' hick towns. It was said to be very popular, perhaps because of the enormous cast iron stove used to heat the shop in winter. It enabled customers to gently toast, even in the middle of winter, as they passed their time in the shop. This newsagent later moved up the street to take the more permanent premises of 34 Main Street and the much loved building was no longer needed.

Jack Scoular and his brother Alex began business with a small cycle shop and expanded to open a garage on the site of where the present day Dykes Chain Saw and Lawnmower Workshop stands. As the mechanised variety of transport grew in importance, Scoular's Garage were the proud possessors of the first petrol pump in the area which was situated on the pavement of Main Street. However, in April 1932 the local Perth Council were less impressed. And they complained that the petrol pump was causing an obstruction likely to cause injury to pedestrians, as they were forced to step out onto the road.

Other services in the village included the carpenter, cartwright and undertakers owned by Donald McBeath at 19 Main Street (in business until the mid-1960s) in later years there also was the joiner's shop at 66 Main Street, originally owned by William Sands and later by Jimmy Forrester. Local tradition asserts that a whisky still, one of many, was situated on this site during Thornhill's 'whisky period'. The still is long gone, but the house's role continued to interest the villagers, as it was used for storage of munitions in World War Two. There was great excitement shortly after the war ended when the bomb disposal, police, etc. suddenly descended on the village. They had come to diffuse a large quantity of arms found abandoned near the house. Fortunately there were no untoward incidents and the excitement was short lived.

In addition to the village shops, the everyday needs of the village were served by mobile services. William McLay, the coal merchant, had his base on The Hill. Coal was brought in by railway to Kippen and it was collected by William with his horse and cart. He then went round the village with his huge Clydesdale horse and cart delivering to his customers. He was in competition with Davie Stewart living at 67 Main Street who ran a second coal business in addition to running a tannery. Fresh milk was also available from the Jamieson's of Norrieston, delivered direct to your door. Their customised cart had a huge tank which was filled with fresh milk daily. Their customers would bring their jugs and containers and fill up from a tap at the back of the tank.

Mrs Agnes McLachlan, who owned a lodging house on The Hill (and lived in a small private part of the building), often came round the village with her 'bowl cart' selling china and bric-a-brac. In addition, John Miller, also from The Hill, operated a cart selling fresh fish (*see Fig. 58 on the following page*).

Carts, Statues, Parrots and Penny Farthings

The use of nicknames has been a tradition in many rural areas of Scotland and Thornhill is no exception. The use of nicknames arose in order to differentiate people when there was a limited number of surnames to be found in the neighbourhood. Furthermore there was

Mary Diggens

Fig. 58 Mr John Miller and his fish cart

a tendency for similar family names to be used from one generation to another. Thornhill had its share of colourful names such as 'Duncan the Reiver', 'Ruskie Rab' (a publican in the Crown Hotel during the mid-18th century), 'Kippen Jock', 'Angus the Leer' (how did he get this name?), 'Penny Jack' (Jack Scoular and his Penny Farthing) and many more. This tradition continues, albeit to a limited extent, into the present day. Many of the characters who bore such nicknames have left a deep impression on the history of the village.

The Scoulars caused a few early gasps with their antics on their bicycles. It was well remembered seeing Jack Scoular hurtling down Bells (The Kippen road) Brae. This is not unusual you may think, but he did it on his penny farthing bicycle, which of course was a fixed wheel and had no brakes. He used his bicycles to good effect in other ways when he set up a mobile smithy, which was basically a bicycle with bellows and other accoutrements. Jack was a well-known practical joker and told of his outing to vote at Doune. Accompanied by Mr Allan, a well-known local artist, they travelled to Doune in style on a motorcycle and sidecar. The Duchess of Atholl was canvassing as the local Conservative candidate but at an opportune moment the two of them slapped a red parking ticket on her limousine and no doubt sat back with glee to watch her response. Her reaction is sadly unrecorded.

The popular Tom Newton was well known for his tendency to walk round the village and the local area singing and playing his violin. In 1930, at the age of 83 years, he was walking back from Kippen when he fell dead from a seizure and the village mourned the loss of a character, liked by all.

He was perhaps the last of a long line of similar characters who enlivened the streets and village life. One of the best known was John Robison, better known as 'Kippen Jock.' (*see Fig. 59*) He had a roaming disposition and went round the village (usually accompanied by a crowd of boisterous youths) with a home-made trolley, made by rigging together two bicycle wheels which ran on a well-worn axle attached to a pair of wheels of different dimensions. The wheels were never straight on his cart because they were in his opinion:

A' the better to cope with the road

Thornhill Commonry and "Kippen Jock."

Fig. 59 Kippen Jock

Jock is posing on the South Common along with his famous cart, although the wheels here seem similar in size. The trees in the background mark the borders of the orchard. Within the boundaries of this orchard stood the last thatched cottage in Thornhill.

Jock, his end hastened by a kick from his horse, died at his home in Hill Street and is buried in Norrieston Churchyard (*see Appendix 1*).

'Kippen Jock' was not far wide of the truth regarding the roads, because they were often in a terrible state. The plight of The Hill has already been mentioned (*see Fig. 60*), but even Main Street was not taken over by the council and surfaced until October 1891. The Hill had to wait until 14 December 1937 and this was only after a long campaign by the parish councillors. Astonishingly when the road was finally taken over, it was with an apology from Perth Council. They had agreed to maintain the road in 1891 along with Main Street but amazingly they had mislaid the minute, or some other internal problem arose. It took 46 years to rectify the mistake. Until the surfaces were made up earlier this century everybody was responsible for their own pavement. Consequently some were flagged, some cobbled, some had chippings and some had nothing.

Walking around the village especially during the long winter's

Fig. 60 The Hill or Hill Street

This street, once a cul-de-sac, has a number of fine 18th-century houses, but the road was not made up until 1937. This photograph is from an earlier period and the state of the road and pavement leaves much to be desired.

nights must have been hazardous. There was little to worry about in terms of traffic but the pavements were excellent for breaking ankles. This was made worse by the fact that there was only one gas light for the village situated outside of the former Crown Hotel. This had the task of lighting all of Main Street. This light was removed when the Crown was converted to a domestic residence.

Thornhill socials were perhaps not on the scale of some of the events of the 19th century but were still popular and well attended. Jack Johnston was the town crier and helped enormously to promote attendance as he paraded through the village making sure that no-one missed the news of the day.

The clubs and societies on offer still formed an impressive list. Active were the Band of Hope (under the indefatigable Mrs Connel), the Nursing Association, a very dynamic Women's Rural Institute, the Church Guild, the Football Club (a thriving and successful female football team was also active), the Curling and Bowling Clubs, the Gun Club, Music Clubs, the Scouts and Guides and many more. Hugely popular whist drives were often held in the Commercial Hotel and were enlivened by a parrot which mimicked everything. History has a strange way of repeating itself when, in 1994, the proprietor at that time arrived home – with a parrot.

There was more visiting entertainment too, such as the dramas put on by the West Highland Players in 1932. In April 1935 Ord Pinder even arrived back on the South Common with his visiting circus. Alas, things rarely went to plan on Ord Pinder's Thornhill visits even though the circus took place as planned. However, it was later reported that Jeannie Harris, whose house backed onto the Common, had complained of Pinder's horses breaking into her garden and doing considerable damage. Mr Pinder was ordered to pay damages.

At this time Mr Featherstone from Glasgow had made a big impact. By January 1934 he had acquired 18 properties in the village and was to purchase even more in the next few years. Not all in the village supported his actions and he was certainly a stern landlord. However, others have thanked him for rescuing some of the older properties that may well have fallen into a state of severe disrepair had he not rehabilitated them. The UF manse (Blair Hill), a listed building of 1848, was bought by him and was re-christened

Fig.61 The former United Free Church manse

The former UFC manse, now called Blair Hill, is a listed building dating from 1848. It was nicknamed 'Featherstone Hall' when Mr Featherstone owned a lot of property in the village in the 1930s.

by the youngsters 'Featherstone Hall' (*see Fig. 61*).

The large beech hedge around the garden caused no problem, and neither did the churchyard situated almost next door. Problems did arise though when Mr Featherstone decided to put some statues in his garden. During the long winter nights the children would quicken their pace slightly as they walked past the churchyard. They relaxed on passing safely, only then to be severely jolted as suddenly they saw black figures, where previously there were none, rearing over the hedge of Featherstone Hall. The statues are no longer present and the Norrieston Corner has returned to its more peaceful state.

Industry and Invention

Village employment was still dominated by farming but there were some alternatives. There was an old smiddy at the extreme west end of the village (*see Fig. 62*) but this was superseded by another small smithy to the west end of Main Street which was to become known as Balmoral Cottage. Next door to it was 'The Palace'. Tradition has it that Queen Victoria, passing through the village on one of her numerous trips to the Trossachs, stopped at this point to get a horse's shoe replaced-hence the significance of the names.

To the east was a further smithy at Corshill Cottage just outside the village. This was the home of the MacFarlanes, so noted for longevity. They were also noted for their skills and several generations of master blacksmiths trained and worked here. Daniel MacFarlane (*see Fig. 63*), the famous centenarian, was also something of an inventor and became recognised worldwide in his field when he invented a system to eliminate dust from alternators. His invention must have cleared the air and the minds of those hereabouts because a few years later, in December 1934, Alexander Moir of Little Ward was delighted to receive a £50 prize from the Highland

Fig. 62 The Old Smiddy

An enhanced photograph dating from 1904 showing the Smiddy at the western end of the village. This building is now demolished. The Aberfoyle road is in the foreground. The eagle eyes of Mr Archie Paterson noticed that the poster at the door advertises Buffalo Bill's Wild West Show, which visited Perth and Stirling on the 5th and 6th of September 1904.

Donald MacFarlane

Fig.63 The Crosshill Smithy 'Gang'

Daniel MacFarlane is to the right of the picture and Sandy MacFarlane,
the last smith to work here, is in the centre of the picture. The smithy
in the background is now converted to provide excellent holiday
accommodation.

Agricultural Society for inventing a roller attachment for mowers.

The Mill at Cessintully (*see Fig. 65*) was also an important local
employer until its closure in 1956. Without a doubt the Mill at
Cessintully is one of the oldest sites in the area but the old building
was mainly demolished in 1853. The new mill was a three storey
building with, for the time, a high technology waterwheel (*see Fig.
64*). Above the mill a lade held back and stored the water. A sluice
from the lade took the water by increased gravitational pressure
over the water wheel and back into the Cessintully Burn. The water
wheel was an overshoot, which means that water hit the top of the
wheel thus transferring power from above. This method was considered to be both more efficient and more powerful.

The mill concentrated on producing rolled oats but was able to
mill just about anything required by local farmers. Work was often
hard and the damp hot conditions made it a health hazard at times.
It was hard on the boots too, as the continually wet floors tended
to rot them all too quickly. When the hammer mills became more

Hamish McLachlan

Fig. 64 The Cessintully Mill Wheel

The huge metal mill wheel is now no longer on this site and the Cessintully Mill, perhaps the oldest continuously settled site in the area, is now a private house.

obtainable after the Second World War it was the beginning of the end for the mill, and today the industrial function has gone.

The magnificent water wheel has also now gone as has the round mill ring for the horses. Even the lade sprung a leak and was often dry in the summer. Nevertheless it is easy to imagine amid the pleasant and tranquil surroundings and where otters frequently visited from the Goodie Burn, what a scene of activity must have existed here for over 600 years.

It had its share of drama but fortunately not of the tragic kind. John Millar, one of the last millers, remembered well when all the produce to be milled was brought in by horse and cart. Sometimes things did not always go to plan, especially where strong-willed horses were concerned. A particular Clydesdale was a model worker whilst his master was watching. On this day the master was distracted and the horse took its chance, decided that work was over for the day and started to make its way home. The owner chased the massive Clydesdale along the road almost as far as the Kirk

Fig. 65 Cessintully Mill

where fortunately he caught the beast; probably just in time before his language earned him a severe reprimand from the minister.

A few years later, on a bitterly cold morning during the Second World War, John lit a fire, as he usually did, using straw and corn husks in a desperate attempt to get warm. As his circulation gradually came back he was amused to see the Army arriving in haste thinking the place was on fire. On perceiving the true situation they retreated, rather embarrassed about their overreaction but perhaps they had been told about the fire at nearby Norrieston Farm in July 1934. The fire which originated in a bothy, quickly spread and destroyed a wing of the house containing the bothy, a scullery and a milk house.

Nineteen thirty four and early 1935 were not good years to remember for some local farmers as they were overshadowed by three dreadful accidents. In April 1934 Angus Ferguson, the farmer of Braendam, became caught in the mechanism of an engine and suffered a double fracture of both legs. By February 1935, two remarkably similar accidents at nearby farms were both to end in loss of life for the poor unfortunates, almost giving truth to the Norrieston legend of death happening in threes.

Indeed life was still hard and officialdom very strict, as a local boy found out in 1933 when he succumbed to temptation and stole a watch from the Corshill Smithy. His punishment was a very hefty fine, far in excess of what he could pay, or 20 days' imprisonment as an alternative.

23

Keep the Home Fires Burning: World War Two

EVENTS IN THE YEARS LEADING UP TO 1939 gave no clue to an impending crisis. Patriotism was rife and in 1934 the massive new trans-atlantic liner, the Queen Mary, had her maiden voyage down the Clyde with three buses full of villagers from Thornhill there to cheer her on. Back in the village, the Amateur Dramatic Society led by Sandy Scoular managed to perform such light hearted sketches as 'The Lunatic And Others' and 'Paddy And The Ghost'. The new Thornhill Jazz Band (of Alex. Miller, Jimmy Douglas and Mhairi Miller) continued to entertain and a village craze for fancy dress showed no sign of abating. For example, on 24 July 1938, a fancy dress parade in aid of the hall extension fund was held on the South Common and was followed by the usual dance in the hall. Winners of the main prizes were; lady's prize to Miss B Williamson (lady in waiting), the lady in a male costume to Nurse MacFarlane, the best comic costume to Messrs. McLachlan, Donaldson and Petrie (The Three Macs) and the children's winner was Miss O McGregor.

Betty Spence

Fig. 66 Jock Miller the cowboy arrives

The usual clubs and societies continued and many, such as the Women's Rural Institute, were positively thriving. A 1938 article in the Stirling Journal on the appalling persecution of Jews in Germany was noted but did not dampen the optimistic attitude. Even an outbreak of typhoid, blamed on watercress, did not cause undue

Betty Spence

Fig. 67 Thornhill fancy dress party

Thornhill society was adept at making its own entertainment, and the
fancy dress party was common and always popular. The photograph
above from the late 1920s gives a flavour of such events.
Left to Right: E. Spence, L. Stewart, J. MacFarlane, P. Ainslie,
D. Stewart, N. MacFarlane.

alarm but the mood began to change in late 1938 and 1939 as the
prospect of war began to loom.

The football club were the first to show the mood change as they
staged their own rehearsal of war with Germany in a match against
Balfron on 25 July 1938 on the South Common. A keenly fought
contest ultimately boiled over and a series of free fights took place
leading to the home spectators invading the pitch. The pitch was
finally cleared and the referee wanted to continue. However, Balfron refused and so the game was abandoned. In a year's time the
whole league was to be postponed as the young people of the area
had an altogether more serious battle to fight.

By March 1939 plans had been put in place and the village was
busy rehearsing black out procedures which were to last almost six
years. April saw the distribution of gas masks to all the villagers.

In September, war with Germany was declared. Almost immediately, the Stirling area received a number of evacuees from Glasgow

and by 7 September 90 evacuees had arrived in the village by bus. They were given tea in the school and then they moved on to their temporary homes in local houses and farms. The school was soon on a double shift with the hours being 9–12 am for locals and 1–4 pm for evacuees. A second supply of evacuees arrived from Glasgow on Thursday 12 October. They came to Doune Station and were conveyed by bus to the school. Many of the evacuees were to stay only a short time. Their parents, mainly from Glasgow, visited them and often decided to take the risks and bring them back home. A few Clydebank parents were to regret that decision, as the blitz was destined to strike their town in the very next year.

Although not strictly an evacuee, Daphne Whibberley, (*nee* Johnston), along with her mother and three sisters, arrived from London on the 2 September to stay with her grandmother Helen Johnston.[60] They went to live in the family home, Albion House on Main Street (*see Fig. 68*)[61] and in total 19 people lived in the house. Daphne well remembered the hardships of rationing, the queues for food and supplies and the excitement of getting a few extra sausages from Gray the butcher. They were not to return to their London home until 1945.

It was realised that despite all the planning no-one actually knew what the procedure was in the event of an Air Raid warning and so the following instructions were transmitted in local newspapers and advertising posters in the village:

> *The warning will be transmitted by the ringing of church bells reinforced by special constables blowing sharp blasts on their whistles. If poison gas is suspected a hand rattle will be used. All people to remain inside until the all clear is sounded*

The blackout was also soon in full force and Mr Carmichael cycled down Main Street ringing his bell and looking for any lights from the darkened windows. As the village did not yet have electricity, oil lamps were the only cause for concern. Fortunately these precautions were never put to the test. However, there were mistakes,

---

60 Personal recollections of Daphne Whibberley (*nee* Johnston).

61 Albion House was then the home of the Johnston family, very well-known and respected Thornhill residents, both then and now.

Fig. 68 Albion House

such as when the Home Guard, based in the Masonic Lodge, had an exercise involving a simulated invasion and the warning bells were rung. Unfortunately no-one told the rest of the village that it was an exercise and for a period of time chaos and confusion ensued.

The confusion that reigned then was as nothing compared to the impact of the small earthquake of February 1940, which shook the village, rattled the windows and convinced most people that the bombing had started. It had not, but Miss Peggy Douglas of Callander Road was facing the real thing. She had joined the ambulance unit based in the Port of London and served throughout the London Blitz. She was commended for great personal bravery and on one occasion she had to deal with casualties at three separate incidents It was stated that she:

> *showed courageous devotion to duty in the face of great*
> *personal danger*

The nearest Thornhill came to being bombed was when a landmine was dropped at nearby Rednock on the Port of Menteith road. In 1941 the village was designated as an official rest centre in the event of severe bombing elsewhere in Scotland and very quickly

Fig. 69 The Crown Coach House

The old coach house behind the former Crown Hotel is now a listed building and may well be one of the original buildings of the village. It had a number of functions in the past including the NCOs' mess in World War Two.

the village had begun to take on the appearance of a military camp. The Cheshire Regiment was billeted in the village with the Commercial Hotel used for the officers and the Crown Hotel used for the NCOs. The WRI was kept busy staffing the soldiers' canteen and organising entertainment for the troops. Behind the former Crown Hotel is the listed old coach house (which could well be an original Thornhill building) now converted to living accommodation but then acting as the NCOs' mess.

The soldier who served as the officers' cook was well remembered but not for his cooking. His red face shone like a beacon and he was none too concerned about hygiene. Perhaps that was why the soldiers dredged the Goodie in search of eels, which were then cooked for them by Helen Johnston in Albion House. The Cheshires soon became well integrated with the village, especially when they organised their picture shows. These affairs were ticket only but it was usually possible to scrounge a ticket off a soldier. On one showing a village youngster whose favourite pastime was to tease the soldiers, failed to get a ticket as a result. His revenge was to disconnect the generator supply to the temporary cinema. He was none too popular with the rest of the villagers for a few days. Needless to say, there was no cinema that night and the young lad in question kept his head down for a few weeks!

The Royal Army Ordnance Corps also had a large presence in the village and both the Hill and the Low Town were used as wagon parks. There were a number of ammunition compounds in the surrounding area, including by the North Common, along the Doune Road and also at Blairhoyle, where remnants of the compound can still be seen built into a wall. Locals watched with amusement as the Home Guard, ordered to defend the ammunition dump on the North Common, decided to dig a slit trench for cover. Unfortunately, the North Common is notorious for its poor drainage. Although it is the home of a number of rare plants it does not make ideal trench country. The Guard found out the hard way and groaned

Hamish McLachlan

Fig. 70 The Home Guard

The Home Guard complete with Pipe Band march down the Main Street. Notice the delight of the children on the right of the picture as they carefully copy the drummers. All the road signs have been removed in order to confuse any German parachutists who might appear in the area.

with frustration as the trench slowly filled with water.

Many of the old Great War soldiers were active in the Home Guard and the reality of the guard was very different from the TV 'Dads Army' cliché. For example it was written that the Home Guard:

presented an inspiring sight, with all looking very fit and smart

Even the schoolchildren formed their own army, complete with pretend officers and NCOs.

The war made a huge impact on all groups in the village. Thornhill was not slow to provide a steady stream of recruits for the war but there were not so many agricultural workers as before and fewer could be spared. The 'Dig for Victory' campaign was well received, as one would expect in an area with such strong agricultural and horticultural tradition. In 1942 a visit to the village was organised by the Women's Rural Institute from the Ministry of Food. A series of cookery demonstrations was given and a talk entitled 'How to make best use of garden produce' was very well received, although most in the village were no slouches at this ancient skill. Probably around the same time, the Department of Agriculture built the The 'Government' Sheds (*see Fig. 71*) on the site of the Orchard. They were to act as a base to assist local farmers to produce crops and vegetables to help the War effort. Around a dozen men were employed as tractor drivers helping with planting, growing and harvesting crops and vegetables. The sheds housed the tractors and implements and there was also a blacksmith's forge where repairs were carried out. The sheds continued even after the war had ended until finally the tractors, implements and equipment were auctioned off on the South Common on the 8 July 1955 and the sheds were bought by Alexander Millar, Haulage Contractor, Thornhill. [62]

The girls and ladies of the village particularly excelled themselves in fund-raising and providing comfort support for the armed services. Very impressive sums of money were raised on a regular basis. The Girl's Guildry regularly toured the houses collecting old teapots, kettles and anything metal which could be reused to support the

---

[62] From an article written for 'Thornhill – Then and Now' (Facebook group) by Archie Paterson, January 2018.

Archie Paterson

Fig. 71 The 'Government' sheds

The sheds prominently feature on the South Common but were originally built to support local farmers during the Second World War. They are on the site of an orchard and the last thatched cottage in the village.

war effort. A constant stream of produce left the village through-out the war. In April 1941 alone the ladies of the village presented to the Red Cross:

- 43 pairs of socks
- 24 body belts
- 2   pairs of gloves
- 1   pair of mittens
- 12 sets of pyjamas
- 5   vests
- 4   shirts

Fund raising was equally impressive. An example was 'Warship Week' in May 1942, opened by A.K. Muir of Blair Drummond. Although over £5000 had already been raised by the village just the week prior, a special effort was still made. There was a procession, led by a Pipe Band followed by the Home Guard and Civil Defence Service, the Special Police, Women's Voluntary Service and Girl's Guildry. After the procession a football match between the local Home Guard and the Royal Army Service Corps took place at Blairhoyle followed by a dance. Other functions during the week included the inevitable fancy dress parade (winners were Mrs McPhail [Highlander] and William Dawson [Victorian lady], and for the children Elma Dick [Dutch girl]), a jumble sale and 2 further concerts and dances. By the end of the week Thornhill had raised over £12,200; a magnificent total. The 'Wings for Victory' week in 1943 raised £17,282 – far in excess of the target and the 'Salute the Soldier' week in June 1944 was equally successful. The target was set at £10,000 but the amount actually raised was £16,250.

The years of war continued to drag on and many anxious families waited for news of their sons from the various fronts. Sadly, tragic news was all too frequent, as four Thornhill soldiers lost their lives during the war and a number of others were severely injured. Peter Mailer was the first fatality of the village when he lost his life in November 1941. He served, as did so many of his predecessors of World War One, with the Black Watch and was part of the 2nd battalion stationed in the Middle East. It was probably during Operation Crusader, an attempt to retake Tobruk which occurred in November 1941 that he lost his life. This bloody engagement saw over 300 British casualties in one hour. Despite the heavy losses and reverses, the battalion moved on to relieve Tobruk. Further sad news came the following year when William Anderson and then Andrew Hutchison were killed. Lance Corporal Alexander Cowan had hoped the war was nearly over in March 1945 but it was not quite early enough for him. He served with the Medical Corps but was killed in the advance into Germany.

It was not just combatants who were to suffer. Reginald Binnie of the Brae of Boquhapple worked as a customs officer in the Malayan Customs Service. Following the Japanese attack on Malaya in September 1942, it was decided to evacuate the civilians with all haste. Reginald's wife Ethel (*nee* Lockerbie) boarded the SS *Kuala* in a bid to escape the Japanese attacks.

While still taking on passengers, SS *Kuala* was attacked by wave after wave of enemy aircraft, killing dozens of passengers. The ship was carrying 600 people, 500 of whom were civilians. Half of these were women and children. Scores were injured by shrapnel fragments and flying glass. As the nurses did their best to bind up the bleeding wounds, the atmosphere was one of utter panic. The ship was then rocked by a massive explosion as the bridge suffered a direct hit and the boiler room caught fire. With the stricken vessel sinking fast, the order came to abandon ship. There were only two lifeboats and not nearly enough lifebelts. Terrified passengers were forced to jump from the blazing ship into the water where a fierce current was sweeping them away from the island and out to the open sea. They hung on to whatever they could, anything that floated, and then the Japanese dive bombers came swooping down and strafed them, hitting the lifeboats and catapulting many of the passengers back into the sea. One of the many to die in this dreadful attack was Ethel Binnie.

Occasionally more cheerful news came through, such as when Donald Beaton was promoted to Sergeant in the RAF and mentioned in dispatches for his bravery in action. Also, Walter Stewart of Slatehaa, serving with the Commandos, was awarded the oak leaf decoration. Many of the wounded were tended in Blair Drummond Auxiliary Hospital and the Girl's Guildry expended a great deal of time in organising diversions for them such as beetle drives, quizzes, etc.

The village had 'done its bit and more' for the war effort and richly deserved the celebrations that occurred in May 1945 on the occasion of VE Day. The village was decorated with flags and bunting throughout. Two effigies of Hitler, one in Hill Street and one on a bonfire on the Common, were burned with glee. A special service in the church was held followed by a very well attended dance in the church hall. The band comprised all local players and three pipers were also present. Just before midnight the whole party, led by the pipers, went to the South Common. A bonfire was lit at one minute past midnight by Private N. MacDiarmid, a serviceman on leave. A quiet prayer was said for all the people who had lost their lives in the war. Then everyone trooped back to the hall for the dancing and celebrations which were to last throughout the night.

24

Postwar Thornhill

THE MODERN HISTORY OF THE VILLAGE IS a task for a future chronicler and is outside the scope of this book. Nevertheless a brief resume of developments may be of interest to the reader.

Following the armistice, for the second time in the 20th century the village had to pick itself up and get back to normal life. The immediate history of the village, post 1945, was mainly concerned with this aim.

Village services still dominated the post war agenda. Fortunately there had been some progress. The new water supply was now in operation and the campaign for bringing electricity to the village, which began before the war, had brought success when street lights were first installed in 1947. It was to take some time before both water and electricity were installed in all the houses.

The Commons were still causing some problems. The council had taken over the South Common with the agreement of the feuars. A similar scheme was rejected for the North Common, despite comments that it was an eyesore, still with a minor gypsy problem and the more serious problem of straying livestock. It was not surprising that it was called an eyesore because at that time the village sewage was directed into its ditches and drains. The animals hardly helped matters. Council minutes for 11 July 1946 complain that cattle had broken into gardens, with cattle and horses from the North Common straying onto the main road. The council agreed to take action on this and also clear out the ditches whose banks had been broken by livestock. Much of the western portion of the Common was cleared and later levelled but had no further development.

The Common today has a very different role in the village. It is rare to find unimproved land near any urban settlements in Scotland and in the North Common Thornhill has an almost unique asset. It is now home to about 150 native plant species and is frequented from time to time by rare birds and animals. Its chief role is acting as a 'lung' for the residents. Whether it is for the children to have open rough land to explore or whether it is for exercising the dog or the horse it is an important open space.

By 1946 the village began its campaign to have a new drainage and sewerage system and the present arrangements came into effect in 1951. It was sorely needed to cope with both existing and new housing. The Main Street had stubbornly stuck to its traditional ways with most houses known by the name of their occupants, either present or past. Locals had no problem with this and the custom is still evident despite all the houses being given numbers in 1950.

Civic pride has already featured in this chronicle and was still manifest in more recent times. A Canadian visitor to the village in 1967 had toured the whole area and wrote that:

Thornhill was the tidiest place we saw, with not as much as a bus ticket to mar the Main Street

Fig. 72 The Crown Hotel, 1956 (now 27, 29 Main Street)

This photograph taken in 1956 shows a neat line in brickwork at the front of the hotel. Note the signs on the front and roof, and also the television aerial, one of the first in the village.

This was encouraging and very much needed in view of the relative poverty still evident in the neighbourhood. By 1979 it was reported that Thornhill had too many substandard houses with 16 either under a demolition order or proposed demolition. The Thornhill Development Plan then came into being to improve the current housing stock and build new houses in gap sites in Low Town and Doig Street. The plan also involved landscaping, an improvement to the sewerage system and the development of a village clinic. The few new houses in the village were in great demand. It would still be very surprising to find so much as a bus ticket littering the street, although it must be said that the frequency of buses does tend to make this even more unlikely!

The population structure has seen changes which reflect modern life. Thornhill could still be regarded as 'on the edge' although it would be stretching the truth to call it remote. Its distance from the central belt makes it possible for residents to follow a commuter lifestyle with many now working in Stirling or further afield. Nevertheless it retains its core of agricultural activity and a country lifestyle. Thornhill lies just outside the recent boundary designation of the new Loch Lomond and the Trossachs National Park. However, it's historic and heritage appeal is now recognised. Its relative lack of change from the initial village foundation in 1696 makes Thornhill, although not unique, very significantly valued. The designation of parts of Thornhill as a conservation area underlines this.

The village is far from a dead commuter town and a resident from 100 years ago would not feel too out of place. Agriculture remains a central part of the local economy with some specialisations. Any visitor to the 'Big Onion Competition' would gasp at the size and quality of the vegetables, and will be left in no doubt that horticulture remains popular and strong.

The growing tourist industry is prominent with many visitors now staying in the village area at the Lion and Unicorn, local bed and breakfast establishments and the Mains Farm Wigwams. The Trossachs Trail, which passes through the village, is likely to increase the popularity of the local area still further. The multiplicity of local clubs and activities remain strong. The online presence of the village, especially through the work of the Thornhill Community Trust, means that interest in the important history and heritage of the village and its surroundings remain robust. The age mix and social harmony together with an active and friendly village environment means that the comments of 'Toledo' made over 100 years ago still apply when he described the village as:

the pleasantest of pleasant villages

Appendix 1

Norrieston Churchyard

In the early 20th century the Reverend George Williams made some observations on some of the older stones in Norrieston Churchyard following on from research by James McGregor in the mid-19th century. The Scottish Genealogical Society continued the study in 1974 but noted that many of the inscriptions were unreadable and some of the stones had been removed when the council took over the churchyard to enable mowing machines to be used. It is therefore worth recording the more interesting stones for posterity although few now remain.

The oldest stone was a rough slab inscribed:

    1675. HER LYS JG. : I.M.

The original benefactor of the land upon which the church and churchyard stands was Gabriel Norrie. Even in the Reverend Williams' time his gravestone was virtually unreadable but what could be made out said:

    HEIR LYES GABRIEL NORRIE OF NORRIESTOUN WHO [   ] THIS LIF
    THE 13 [   ] PTR..81 AND OF HIS AGE F 47.

    HE EVER WYS AND PRUDENT WAS

    AT HOM ABROOD AS WIS MEN KNAWS

    G.N. & U. [   ]

Nearby is the gravestone of his wife:

    MARGARET FORRESTER, LADY NORRIE, WHO DEPARTED ...

The rest of the stone is underground. There were at least five or six other stones dating from the seventeenth century such as:

HER LYS A.M.

LS. MG

HEIR LYES SAMUEL MARJORIBANKS WHO DEPARTED THIS LIFE THE
14TH DAY OF MARCH AND OF HIS AGE 28, 1690

Our forefathers took some comfort from the lyrical inscriptions
often carved upon their close relatives' gravestones. It is always so
poignant to hear of the tragedies, often involving young children,
which stared into the faces of our ancestors so often:

ANDREW SYMERS AND ELIZABETH SMITH WHERE LYES INTERD
ELIZABETH AND ANDREW AND JEAN AND ALEXANDER SYMERS WHO
DIED YOUNG, CHILDREN OF THEIRS
HEIR LYES FOUR BLOSSOMS EARLY PUED
EVER THEY CAME TO THEIR PRIEM
THEIRFOR DO YOU IMPROVE WEAILL
WHILE YOU HAVE PRECIOUS TIME   1770

A later Sommers' grave has an excellent pun:

WHO NEEDS A TEACHER TO ADMONISH HIM
THAT FLESH IS GRASS, THAT EARTHLY THINGS ARE MISTS?
WHAT ARE OUR JOYS BUT DREAMS, AND WHAT OUR HOPES
BUT GOODLY SHADOWS IN THE SUMMER'S CLOUD

The modest grave of George McKerracher (hanged for forgery) and
Agnes Fisher lay nearby (although the stone has gone), as still does
the grave of Duncan McLachlan, late of Macrieston, who died in
1832. Duncan was the son of 'Duncan the Reiver'. We know little
about him, but it is said that another of Duncan's sons went missing
in the moss and his body was finally found by means of a dream
of his sister that correctly identified his location. A rather sombre
message lay on the gravestone of John Smith:

HEARE LAYS THE CORPS OF JOHN BOWIE SMITH, WHO DEPARTED
THIS LIFE NOV 21ST 1791, AGED 21 YEARS

On the reverse side could be read:

O MORTAL MAN AS YOU PASS BY
ON THIS TOMBSTONE CAST YOUR EYE
WHAT YOU ARE NOW SO ONCE WAS I
MY GLASS WAS RUN AND YOURS IS RUNNING
PREPARE FOR DEATH, JUDGEMENT IS COMING

The Spittal family have a stone which records their names and goes on to read:

STOP STRANGER HERE AND VIEW
THY PICTURED FATE HOWEVER HON[OR'D]
OR HOWEVER GREAT ALL CONQUERING
DEATH WITHOUT DISTINCTION BRINGS
ON EQUAL FOOTING HUMBLE MEN
AND KINGS. ON FAITH AND VIRTUE
THEN YOUR HOPE MUST REST
BEING NUMBERED WITH THE TRULY BEST

A very touching inscription recorded the grave of Isabel Ramsay of Thornhill, who died aged 18 on the 4 July 1799:

BOQUHAPPLE BRED ME, LEARNING BROUGHT ME, AND NORRIESTON
CAUGHT ME. LABOUR PRESSED ME, AND SICKNESS DISTRESSED ME,
AND DEATH OPPRESSED ME, AND THE GRAVE POSSESSED ME. GOD
FIRST GAVE ME, CHRIST DIED TO SAVE ME, THE EARTH DID CRAVE
ME AND HEAVEN WOULD HAVE ME. BOTH OLD AND YOUNG AS YOU
HERE PASS ME BY, I DESIRE WHILE YOU AE ALL IN LIFE, TO THINK
ON THE STATE IN WHICH I NOW LY, FOR AS YOU ARE SO ONCE WAS
I, AND NOW IN THE GRAVE HERE LY

The MacLarens' of Middleton have a large stone with many of their family recorded including the famous architect and designer of the village of Fortingall, James Marjoribanks MacLaren.

Appendix 2

The Thornhill Piper

Once a familiar sight on entering Thornhill, this poem was written
to mark the sad occasion when the piping figure was taken away.

The ae leggit minstrel wha cheered Thornhill
The sough o' his reeds O, wae's me is still
Fareweel to the piper, they've ta'en him awa
Drone, chanter, bag, bonnet, feather an a'
Fareweel, fareweel to oor piper

The laddies threw stanes as they went by the hoose
Yet he never complained, or let his temper loose;
Wi a body roun' a fav'rite was he
we likit himsel' an' his sweet melodie
Fareweel, fareweel to oor piper

He aye played the tunes his hearers thocht best
pathetic or merry according to taste
An tho' some didna hear the music he played
Yet fretfu' remarks he never aince made
Fareweel, fareweel to oor piper

They've ta'en him awa to a better place
Whar' we trust he'll be treated wi' kindly grace
Nae mair can the folks o' Thornhill dae
Than salute oor auld frien' wi R.I.P.
Fareweel, fareweel to oor piper

Anon.

Appendix 3

Volunteers for active service from Thornhill and District in October 1914

(They were to be joined by many more as the war progressed)

Malcolm Baird	Royal Fusiliers
Colin Baird	Black Watch
John Bremner	Argyll and Sutherland Highlanders
James Brown	Black Watch
John Buchanan	Black Watch
James Buchanan	Black Watch
Alex Buchanan	Black Watch
John Campbell	Seaforth Highlanders
Robert Donaldson	Cameronians
Gilbert Hamilton	Highland Light Infantry
Milton Hamilton	Highland Light Infantry
John Hay	Black Watch
William Miller	Cameron Highlanders
Charles Moir	Black Watch
James Montgomery	Scottish Horse
Joseph Murray	Scottish Horse
Hugh Murray	Seaforth Highlanders
William Murray	5th Dragoon Guards
Alexander McDonald	Argyll and Sutherland Highlanders
Archibald McDonald	Scottish Horse
John McLachlan	Black Watch
John McKinley	Black Watch
Alexander McKenzie	Royal Navy
Gabriel Newton	Black Watch
John Rae	Argyll and Sutherland Highlanders
Peter Sinclair	Argyll and Sutherland Highlanders

Appendix 4

Kippen Jock

A poem to celebrate 'Kippen Jock' written by a person who knew him well

When Kippen Jock drave oot his yoke
Wi' her'n an' haddies laden
It was a joy to man and boy,
Douce matron and fair maiden;
But on that yoke, the canny folk,
Wad ne'er their ainsel's lippen
th'o a' agreed, Jock was, indeed,
the uncrowned king o' Kippen.

When Kippen Jock gaed on the troke,
wi' sheltie aft rebellin',
The baudrons kent the gate he went,
an' after him gaed yellin',
The wheels ungreased, baith whined and wheezed,
An' set the peesweeps skirlin',
till echoes broke on Kilmadock,
Syne back again on Stirlin'.

When Kippen Jock assessed his stock,
While on their highroad bauchlin',
The wheels had ne'er been meant to pair, An fearsomely gaed
  shauchlin'.
The sheltie, tae, had ne'er a shae
an' stauchered in an odd way;
Sae wheels an' beast could wale, at least
The best bits o' the roadway.

When Kippen Jock o' riches spoke,
Twas never o' his ain gear;
For fortune aye bade him 'goodbye',
An passed him like a reindeer;
But still apace, he did her chase,
Yet what could be the sequel?
Jock's chariot, an' a' whatnot,
Were tae the task unequal.

When Kippen Jock, ae mornin' woke
Intil his breeks he sprauchled,
But plainly saw an end to't a',
An' couldna mair be trauchled.
For yokes an' men gang doon, an' then,
They canna mair be mended.
Sae this, I fear, like Jock's career,
Maun be untimely ended.

Anon.

Appendix 5

The Black Swans

The local ministers enjoyed a high profile in the village but the villagers were certainly not averse to subjecting them to mild teasing if the opportunity arose. The 'black swans' refer to the Church of Scotland minister the Rev Mitchell and the United Free Church minister the Rev Williams, both practising in the village in the early years of the 20th century. The poem, reputedly written by Jock Ferguson, the proprietor of the Crown Hotel, refers to the time when the ministers fell through the ice of the curling pond situated on the Lug in the North Common.

A pair o' swans fell on the 'lug'
and spoilt oor pond for curlin'
They spread their wings oot raither wide,
and through the ice gaed birlin'

You're aware they've awa' necks
Thats what kept them fleatin'
Had anither minute passed
They were at the bottom

A lucky thing that I was there
I couldna' hae been faster
had it not been for my pluck
Twa kirks withoot a Pastor

Ane was short an' ane was tall
The wee ane got the best o't
The wee ane landed tae the neck
The big ane got the rest o't

When we get them tae the shore
Hoo comical thay lookit
They shood their feathers in the sun
For they were fairly dreekit

The only cure we could apply
Altho' a little risky
Was Dr. William's Pink pills
And Mitchell's Irish Whiskey

When they found safe,
they made for hame
But took anither track,
Instead o' merchin east the toun
They slippit roon' the back

Appendix 6

Listed buildings in the Thornhill and Blair Drummond Area

Blair Drummond
Blair Drummond House and Ancillaries
 (11 listed, including 7 List B)
Blair Drummond Corner
Blair Drummond Corner, Sawmill
Parish Church, Kincardine
Kincardine Manse
Kincardine School
Kincardine Graveyard
Blair Drummond School

In Thornhill
Hillview, Thornhill
Norrieston House and Heatherlea Thornhill
Barn at Rear of Menteith House Main Street, Thornhill
37, 39 Main Street Thornhill
Crown Hotel, Main Street, Thornhill (now private residence)
Blairhill, Main Street, Thornhill
Blairhoyle Masonic Lodge Main Street Thornhill
Norrieston Church Thornhill

Netherton Bridge Over Goodie Water
East Moss-Side Bridge Over Goodie Water
Muschet Tombstone, Burnbank
Loch-Hills Cottage
Craighead, Farmhouse

Buildings-at-risk register
Tannery Managers House, Thornhill

Appendix 7

Populations of Kincardine and Kilmadock

Year	Kincardine	Kilmadock
1755	1250	2730
1801	2212	3044
1811	2419	3131
1821	2388	3150
1831	2456	3752
1841	2232	4055
1851	1993	3659
1861	1778	3312
1871	1484	3170
1881	1351	3012
1891	1277	2760
1901	1308	2705
1911	1150	2428
1921	1140	2363
1931	1126	2282
1941	1080	2054
2011	1148	2375

Appendix 8

Elegy ... on the deplorable Death of Margaret Hall

barbarously murder'd by her Husband Nicol Muschet of Boghall, Mondays Night the 17 October 1720, in the 17th Year of her Age

All Hearts be swell'd with Grief, with Tears all Eyes,
Lament with Sighs and penitential Crys ...
Harmless and Young, a fond and loving Wife,
Dies by her bloody Husband's murd'ring Knife.
In silence of the Night, when good Men sleep,
And Satan and his Sons their Revels keep :
Th' inhumane Wretch, with soft decoying Talk,
Leads forth his loving Spouse to take a Walk ;
She, (Fair without, and Innocent within)
Dream'd of no Danger, nor th' approaching Sin ;
Hangs round his Waste, Kind are the Words she speaks,
Printing deep Kisses on the Traitor's Cheeks.
Love drove her with him to the fatal Spot,
Where he and Satan who had form'd the Plot,
Throws down the trembling Prey, and cuts her Throat.
Oft hath that Place been wet with humane Gore,
But never saw so black a Crime before.
There he displays the Implement of Death,
Pale were her Looks, and short her dying Breaty,
When she beholds her Husband's naked Knife,
She crys, dear Nicol, will you kill your Wife?
Ah me! Is this the Kindness that ye shew
To her, who left her Father's House for you?
My Words shall with Zjpporas Speech agree,
A bloody Husband, have you prov'd to me.
Soaking with Blood, he left his breathless Wife,
Return'd with Joy, and hug'd the murd'ring Knife,
Men shall Record his Punishment and Shame,
Children unborn shall Curse the Wretche's Name:

Nicol Muschet's co-conspirator James Campbell of Burnbank was charged with ravishing Margaret Hall, administering poison to her and falsehood in the conspiracy to murder her. He was sentenced to transportation and the following poem is attributed to him.

What hellish fury mov'd me
To do this bloody wrong?
Both whoredom and adultery,
And murder that I've done.
All wickedness I did contrive,
Which I did carry on,
But by the Lords I am sentenc'd
To some plantation.
I was store-master made
Of that great castle strong,
A very good creditable post,
But there I did much wrong;
I wronged King and country both,
Good arms I put away,
And kept the money to myself,
Ah! Cunning villainy.

Nicol Mushet I drew on
All for his golden store,
To murder his dear wife,
And lay her in her gore.
I told him to contrive her death,
If gold he'd give me free,
The like you never heard before,
Such bloody villainy.

James Mushet and his wife
Was guiltier than me,
Of that great horrid murder For which Boghall did die;
They gave his lady poison strong,
And a hammer they did get,
To meet his lady in the closs,
And knock her in the head.

My table with fine dishes,
Yonder I'll never see,
Nor yet my bonny lasses,
That's been so kind to me.
What will they say when I am gone?
Oh! How they'll sigh and moan,
Cause I am o'er the ocean sent
To a plantation

Now, farewell to all friends,
For I must leave the shoar,
O'er the raging seas,
Where foaming billows roar.
Why did I act such villainy,
To bring myself in thrall?
I caused Muschet for to kill
His wife, young Margaret Hall.

Bibliography and Further Reading

Abbreviations

NRS	National Records of Scotland, Edinburgh
CRA	Central Region Archives, Stirling
DGNHAS	Dumfries and Galloway Natural History and Antiquities Society
PA	Perth Archives
FNH	Forth Naturalist and Historian
ER	The Exchequer Rolls of Scotland
RCAHMS	Royal Commission on the Ancient and Historic Monuments of Scotland

Spelling

Many of the older references, especially placenames and personal names, have varied spellings. To avoid confusion I have used modern spellings unless by doing so I believe that it would undermine the authenticity or understanding of the original source material.

General Comments

The first edition of this work was not fully notated in an attempt to make it more readable and accessible. Whilst it is my intention to avoid this book being too dry I have referenced and used footnotes where it is deemed appropriate. The source material used falls into three distinct categories. The first is the traditional historical reference, whether primary or secondary. The second is the extensive use of personal diaries and newspaper articles for contemporary accounts. The third is taken from personal recollections and memories.

To assist any future researcher I have highlighted in bold those texts and sources which have been of particular importance in compiling this history.

Sources

Anderson, A.O. *Scottish Annals from English Chronicles: A.D. 500 to 1286*. Edinburgh, 1908.

Anderson, A.O. (Ed). *Early Sources of Scottish History, A.D. 500 to 1286*. 2 vols., Edinburgh, 1922.

Archaeological Field Survey Society of Antiquaries of Scotland, *The Archaeological Sites and Monuments of Stirling District*, 1979.

Balfour, P.J. (Ed.). *Scots Peerage*, vol. VI, Edinburgh, 1909.

Barrow, G.W.S. *Robert the Bruce and the Community of the Realm of Scotland*. 3rd ed., Edinburgh, 1988.

Barrow, G.W.S. *The Kingdom of the Scots*. 2nd ed., Edinburgh, 2003.

Barrow, G.W.S., *Kingship and Unity: Scotland 1000-1306*. 2nd ed., Edinburgh, 2003.

Bartlett, R. *The Making of Europe: Conquest, Colonization, and Cultural Change, 959–1350*. London, 1993.

Barty, A.B. *The History of Dunblane*. Reprint, Stirling, 1994.

Bennet, R. *Capital Punishment and the Criminal Corpse in Scotland 1740–1834*. PhD Thesis, 2016.

Boardman, S. *The Early Stewart Kings: Robert II and Robert III*. East Linton, 1996.

Boardman, S. 'The Gaelic World and the Early Stewart Court' in Mìorun Mór nan Gall, 'The Great Ill-Will of the Lowlander'? *Lowland Perceptions of the Highlands, Medieval and Modern*, edited by D. Broun and M. MacGregor, University of Glasgow, 2007.

Boyle, S. and Macinnes, L. *The Historic Landscape of Loch Lomond and the Trossachs*. RCAHMS and Historic Scotland, 2000.

Broun, D., Finlay, R.J., and Lynch, M. *Image and Identity: The Making and Remaking of Scotland Through the Ages*. Edinburgh, 1999.

Brown, K.M. *et al* eds. *The Records of the Parliaments of Scotland to 1707*. St. Andrews, 2007–18.

Brown, M. *The Wars of Scotland 1214–1371*. Edinburgh, 2004.

Brown, P.H. *Early Travellers in Scotland*. Edinburgh, 1981.

Browne, M. and Mendum, J. *Loch Lomond to Stirling: A landscape fashioned by Geology*. Scottish Natural Heritage, 1997.

Cadel, H.M. *Story of the Forth*. James MacLehose and Sons, Glasgow, 1913.

Campbell J. *The Sorrowful Lamentation of James Campbell of Burnbank*, in Chalmers, G. *Caledonia: or a historical and topographical account of North Britain*. 7 vols + index, Vol. 1. Paisley, 1887–94.

Carver, E. *Inchmahome Priory and the Lake of Menteith*. Historic Scotland, 2003.

Census records, NRS, various.

Cess books, PA, 1703–19.

Cook W. B. *The Stirling Antiquary*, Reprinted from "The Stirling Sentinel," 1888–1906. Cook & Wylie, Stirling, 1904.

Corbett, L., and Dix, N.J. (eds.). *Central Scotland: Land, Wildlife, People*. Stirling, 1993.

Cowbrough J.G. *Lodge Blairhoyle no. 792*. 1995.

Cunninghame Graham R.B. *Notes on the District of Menteith*. 2nd ed, Stirling, 1907.

Devine, T. *The Scottish Nation, 1700–2000*. Penguin, 1999.

Dixon, G.A. 'The Founding of Thornhill, 1696,' FNH 18, 1995.

Dixon, G.A. *Gartmore*. FNH 26, 2003.

Dixon, P. *Puir Labourers and Busy Husbandmen: the Countryside of Lowland Scotland in the Middle Ages*. Edinburgh, 2002.

Drysdale W. *Old Faces, Old Places and Old Stories of Stirling*, 1898. Ulan reprint, 2012.

Drysdale W. *Auld Biggins of Stirling*, 1904. Reprint Kessinger Publishing, 2010. DGNHAS Transactions, 1918–19.

Duncan, A.A.M. *Scotland: The Making of the Kingdom*, Edinburgh, 1975.

Dundas, J.C. & Hutchison, A.S. 'The Parish of Kincardine' in

Gaelic speakers in Medieval Menteith. PhD thesis, University of Glasgow, 2011.

McOwan, R. 'A Walk Through the Moss'. Scots Magazine, 121, 1984.

Main L. *Excavations of Fairy Knowe, Buchlyvie*. FNH vol. 3, 1978.

Marshall W. *Historic Scenes in Perthshire*. Oliphant, Edinburgh, 1880.

Mitchell S. and Mitchell J. F. Monumental *Inscriptions (pre 1855) in South Perthshire*. Scottish Genealogy Society, Edinburgh, 1974.

Murray W.H. *Rob Roy MacGregor*, Canongate, Edinburgh, 1995.

Muschet N. *The Confession, &c., of Nicol Muschet, of Boghall: Containing a Brief Narrative of His Life, and a Full Account of the Contrivance and Perpetration of His Crime*. Oliver and Boyd, Edinburgh, 1818.

Napier M. *Memoirs of John Napier of Merchiston*. Blackwood, Harvard, 1834.

Neville, C.J. *Native Lordship in Medieval Scotland: the Earldoms of Strathearn and Lennox, c.1140–1365*. Four Courts Press, Dublin, 2005.

NSA, *New Statistical Account of Scotland*. Blackwood, Edinburgh, 1836.

Nicolaisen, W. F. H. *Scottish Place-Names*. John Donald, Edinburgh, 2001.

Nimmo, W. *General History of Stirlingshire 1777*, 3rd edition, R. Gillespie, 1880.

Norrieston *Kirk Session records*. CRA, various.

Norrieston *UF Kirk Session records*. CRA, various.

Page, R. 'Gateway to the North: I Roman Roads and Early Routes, Ancient Drove and Military Roads'. FNH 31, 35–59, 2008.

Ramsay, J. *Scotland and Scotsmen in the Eighteenth Century, from the MSS of John Ramsay Esq. of Ochtertyre*, ed. A. Allardyce. Edinburgh, 2 vols., 1888.

RCAHMS. *The Archaeological Sites and Monuments of Stirling District.* Central Region, Edinburgh, 1979.

RCAHMS. *The Historic Landscape of Loch Lomond and the Trossachs.* Edinburgh, 2000.

Robertson, J. *General View of the Agriculture in the Southern Districts of the County of Perth.* London, 1794.

Roger, C. *A Week at Bridge of Allan.* Black A. & C., Edinburgh, 1853.

Ross, I.S. *Lord Kames and the Scotland of his day.* Clarendon Press, Oxford, 1972.

Sanderson, M.H.B. *Scottish Rural Society in the Sixteenth Century.* Edinburgh, 1982.

Sasines, Register of. CRA, Various.

SNH. *Loch Lomond and the Trossachs landscape character assessment.* Scottish Natural Heritage commissioned report no.093, 2005.

Scott, W. *Rob Roy.* Hardpress, 2016.

Sibbald, Sir R. *History and Description of Stirlingshire 1707.* Stirling, 1892.

Sinclair Sir J. ed. The Old Statistical Account of Scotland, Edinburgh, 1791-99.

Skene, W.F. *Celtic Scotland* III. Edinburgh, 1880. Slater, directory, 1860.

Smith, D.E. & Holloway, L.K. '*The Geomorphological Setting of Flanders Moss*'. FNH, 23, 2000.

Stevenson D. *The Hunt for Rob Roy.* John Donald, Edinburgh, 2004.

Stewart James. *Settlements of Western Perthshire*, 1990.

Stirling Antiquary vol. 1 various articles, 1893.

Stirling Journal and Advertiser, 1830–1960.

Stirling Observer, 1836–1986.

Stuart J & others. *ER, The Exchequer Rolls of Scotland, ed., 1878–1908.*

Thompson, E. P. *The Making of the English Working Class.* Penguin. 1991.

Thomson, A. *Callander through the Ages*. Callander, 1985.

Timms, D.W.G. (ed.) *The Stirling Region*. University of Stirling, 1974.

Tyler W. *Military Roads of Scotland*. 1976.

Valuation Rolls, West Perthshire, PA, Various.

Wallace, James Mackenzie, *The cheap press in Scotland 1680–1820. A True and Genuine Copy of the Last Speech, Confession and Dying Words of Nicol Muschet of Boghall, Esq; who was executed at Edinburgh 1721 for the horrid and bloody murder of his own wife, on the foot of the Duke's Walk, within the King's-Park, near the Abby of Holy-Rood-House; being one of the greatest, and most penitent speeches ever was published*. McGill University, Montreal, Dec. 2014.

Watson, F. *Flanders Moss – The Historical Background*. Scottish Natural Heritage, 2001.

Watt, D.E.R. and Murray, A.L. (eds.), 2003, *Fasti Ecclesiae Scoticanae ad annum 1638*.

Webster, *A Census of Scotland*. Scottish History Society, 1755.

Whyte I. *Scotland before the Industrial Revolution*. 1995.

Williams G., Rev. *Original Manuscripts c/o* R. Dick, Various.

Websites

Forth Naturalist and Historian

http://www.fnh.stir.ac.uk/journal/back_issues/index.php

Thornhill Conservation Area appraisal

https://www.stirling.gov.uk/__documents/infrastructure-delivery/
thornhill-con-area-app.pdf

History

https://www.scran.ac.uk/

https://canmore.org.uk/

https://www.historicenvironment.scot/archives-and-research/archives-
and-collections/canmore-database/

https://www.nrscotland.gov.uk/files//research/census-records/websters-
census-of-1755-scottish-population-statistics.pdf

https://digital.nls.uk/broadsides/view/?id=15617

http://www.visionofBritain.org.uk

https://scotlandsplaces.gov.uk/digital-volumes/historical-tax-rolls/
hearth-tax-records-1691-1695/hearth-tax-records-perthshire-volume-1

http://lodgeblairhoyle.co.uk/pdf/The_Blairhoyle_Connection.pdf

http://www.tartansauthority.com/global-scots/new-zealand/the-
founding-of-dunedin/

Records of the Parliaments of Scotland to 1707: http://www.rps.ac.uk

Muschet Murder: https://digital.nls.uk/broadsides/view/?id=15617
www.clanntuirc.co.uk/JSNS/V8/JSNS8%20McNiven.pdf

Slave Ownership: http://www.ucl.ac.uk/lbs/

Witches Database: www.shca.ed.ac.uk/Research/witches

Archaeology

http://www.rcahms.gov.uk

Genealogy

The Doig Family Society: https://www.doig.net/Genealogy.html

Biography

John Napier (1885–1900): https://en.wikisource.org/wiki/Napier,_John_ (DNB00)
https://www.scotsman.com/lifestyle/napier-s-wizard-roots-1-465274

The James M MacLaren Society: https://jmmaclaren.org

Letters of Ramsay of Ochtertyre: https://digital.nls.uk/scottish-history-society-publications/browse/archive/126160620#?c=0&m=0&s=0&cv=0&xywh=-1426%2C-226%2C3727%2C4515

Dictionary of National Biography: www.oxforddnb.com

INDEX

C

G

H

L

M

P

R